WE LOVE YOU, MATTY
MEETING DEATH WITH FAITH

Tad Dunne, Ph.D.

Death, Value and Meaning Series
Series Editor: John D. Morgan

Baywood Publishing Company, Inc.
AMITYVILLE, NEW YORK

Copyright © 2000 by Baywood Publishing Company, Inc., Amityville, New York. All rights reserved. Printed in the United States of America on acid-free recycled paper.

Library of Congress Catalog Number: 99-046089
ISBN: 0-89503-203-1 (Paper)

Library of Congress Cataloging-in-Publication Data

Dunne, Tad, 1938-
   We love you, Matty : meeting death with faith / Tad Dunne.
      p. cm. - - (Death, value, and meaning series)
   Includes bibliographical references and index.
   ISBN 0-89503-203-1 (pbk.)
     1. Death- -Religious aspects. 2. Ventresca, Matty. I. Title. II. Series.

BL504.D835 1999
291.2'3 21- -dc21   99-046089

The author and publisher gratefully acknowledge permission for use of the following material:

Gilgamesh. Copyright © 1970 by Herbert Mason. Reprinted by permission of Houghton Mifflin Co. All rights reserved.

The Wisdom of Laotse, translated by Lin Yutang. Copyright © 1948, The Modern Library, New York. Selection from Book Five, "The Conduct of Life," Section 50, reprinted by permission.

Excerpt from *The Jerusalem Bible,* Copyright © 1966 by Darton, Longman & Todd, Ltd. and Doubleday, a division of Bantam Doubleday Dell Publishing Group, Inc., reprinted by permission.

The Upanishads. Trans. Juan Mascaro. Copyright © 1965. Penguin, UK. Excerpt from "Chandogya Upanishad," § 8.1 reprinted by permission.

The Path of Purification. Copyright © 1979 by Bhadantacarya Buddhaghosa. Paragraphs 15 and 41 reprinted by permission of Buddhist Publication Society, Inc., Sri Lanka.

The Bhagavad Gita, translated by Eliot Deutsch. Copyright © 1968, Henry Holt and Company, Inc. Sections XVIII: 63-66; VII: 24-30; VIII: 12-16 reprinted by permission.

In Memory of
Leo Lackamp
1933-1993

Table of Contents

Preface vii

Prolog 1
The story of Matty Ventresca's life and death.

Chapter 1: The Myths about Death 7
A first step in reflecting on death is to ensure that we envision it as a mystery. Several myths, unfortunately, tend to obliterate that vision.

Chapter 2: Our Many Voices 23
A second step in reflecting on death is to notice how people of other cultures think very differently about it. This can help us stand back and take a more objective look at our own views.

Chapter 3: The Image of God in Death 51
If God is Lord over Death, then Death is God's idea for sharing divine life with us. This means reconsidering more simplistic views of God.

Chapter 4: The Law of Care 85
From a scientific point of view, there is a law in the universe that accounts for the emergence of care. It also accounts for death and helps us understand what immortality must be.

Chapter 5: Voices of Redemption 113

> *From a theological point of view, there are both false and true voices about how God redeems us. The true voices make it clear that death is not the enemy.*

Chapter 6: Walking in the Shadow of Death 131

> *From a practical point of view, we need to know how to live with death in mind. This includes the deaths in every day as well as our physical deaths.*

Chapter 7: Meeting Death with Faith 161

> *The kind of faith necessary to meet death is surprisingly universal and yet beguilingly ordinary.*

Sources 171

> *A list of the major sources mentioned or used.*

Index 177

Preface

Matty Ventresca died when he was nine years old.

The death of any nine-year-old is tragic, of course. Matty never had the chance to experience the full richness of the world, never knew sexual intimacy, never brought forth children of his own, never learned a trade, never learned how to converse about the deeper dimensions of love, work, community, war, politics, or death. Yet his life had a richness: Born with a damaged heart, Matty was told that he would die young. He lived in death's shadow in a way that contains a lesson for anyone, adults as well as children. It is a lesson on how we might meet death.

Matty's refreshingly innocent trust in God and his calm fearlessness in the face of death raise an important question for all of us. Is the fearlessness of children in the face of death just naive? Or did Matty have the bare essentials of a faith we should all have? Had he lived to adulthood, would he have rejected his boyhood faith in order to make room for a more mature version? Or can we find in this boy the kind of faith we need to live—and die—as adults?

These are difficult questions because "death" means different things to different people. Just think of the variety of views about death that we can find in the classical sacred texts—the Hebrew Bible, the Christian New Testament, the Muslim Koran, the Hindu Katha Upanishad and the Bhagavad Gita, Buddhist sacred texts, the Tibetan Book of the Dead, the Egyptian Book of the Dead, Plato's accounts of the teaching of Socrates, the Greek myths of Psyche and Eros, the teachings of Confucius, the Mesopotamian Epic of Gilgamesh, and hundreds of myths about death found among American and Australian aborigines. (We will review some of these in Chapter 2.) Some deny an afterlife and others do not. Some believe that death beckons us to improve the world, while others think death teaches us to leave things be.

But what makes the question even more difficult is that new questions about death have come up that the old teachings are unable to answer. Not one of these classical texts above was aware of Freud's work on psychological disease, of Marx's work on the economic forces underlying unhappiness, of the work of Dilthey, Hegel, Toynbee, and others on how historical processes settle the fate of millions. None of the them paid as close attention to the language we use to talk about death as linguist analysts do today.

We don't need to be experts in these new areas to experience their impact. We have grown up talking about life and death in ways unforeseen by anyone a half a millennium ago. We divide up the psychological process of dying into stages. We measure the fullness of life by a GNP. We discuss health care plans that lengthen life's duration and deepen its quality. We debate the morality of capital punishment. We speak of a "denial of death" that constricts our outlook on life.

How might faith enter these discussions of the psychological, economic, and cultural forces that have shaped how we think about death? Some may say that faith speaks its own eternally valid language. They point to ancient, revered texts as the basis of their faith. But just think of what happens when the old teachings need to be translated into a different language. Translators need to choose words in the new language that adequately convey the ideas in the old. But how do they choose among several words, each with nuances shaped by centuries of usage? They have no classical texts that give them directions on translations. No, we choose translators who themselves are men and women "of faith"—meaning there's something in their hearts and minds that guides how they read, translate, and speak. That's the "faith" we need to talk about.

Likewise, some may say that the essential answers were in the pronouncements of authorities. But this holds true at best for the questions of that day. Today we have new questions. And today we have women and men living in death's shadow with a faith shaped by more than external authorities. They carry something by which they choose which authorities have genuine authority. That's the "faith" we need to talk about.

So let us not think of faith as the beliefs of a religious community, the collection of truths written down, the stories of how the community began, or the teachings of the community's leaders. Let us think of faith as something in the heart, something *by which* we decide which community to join, *by which* we judge certain truths to be worthy of belief, *by which* we honor a community's origins, *by which* we listen to leaders with a careful ear.

Faith is an eye for what is good. This faith values certain elements of life without being able to prove, even to oneself, that one's stance toward death is "correct." It is this prior faith that sees what doctrines of "the faith" are worth holding and what leaders are worth following. It is this prior faith that leads believers of every religion to call certain texts "sacred" and to name certain ways of living "holy." It is to this prior faith that we look for enlightenment about death.

This faith, this eye for what is good, is an eye that depends not on logic but on care and affection. It makes value judgments based on a felt inner harmony with those with whom we share love, and not on any intellectual deduction from principles or scientific proofs. Just as a friendship or a family harmony is the touchstone on which we evaluate what people say and do (including what *we* say and do), so being in love with God has this faith as its first fruits.

So we could ask our question about how faith helps us meet death in different words: "What does being in love with the divine tell us about death and dying in today's world?"

To answer this, we must be careful not to get abstract and general. Theories and logic tend to turn thought cold. This is why I want to keep Matty in mind as we think about how to meet death with the eyes of a faith that springs from love. I am concerned that you, the reader, remember how personal and unique each person's death is. As you read on, I hope you will experience some feelings about death, not just thoughts. These feelings will range from fear about your own death—or the death of someone you love—to deep appreciation for one boy who met death with an honorable faith.

One of the most significant achievements of the sciences is the requirement that all participants reveal the experiences and questions that shape their particular approach to their subject. Without this revelation, it would be impossible for readers to make good judgments on what fresh viewpoints a writer brings and what unconscious biases may be at work. Readers interested in my sources will find them listed, by chapter, in the last section, "Sources."

More generally, however, let me state a few facts about my background. I am a Roman Catholic. I now have views on life and death that are quite different from what I was taught as a child and disturbingly different from what is being taught by the Catholic Church today. I am a male, interested in art, medical ethics, and theology. I am also a former Jesuit, a priest, drawn to marriage by a gift of love from above. These particularities might explain why I ask the questions I do. At the same time, in writing this book I have become acutely aware of how my particularities carry many presumptions about how the world works and about the place of religion in human affairs. So, while I've made efforts to root out these unwarranted assumptions, I have little doubt that others remain. I can only hope that readers will find that my perspective will help them deal with their particular questions, and that any bias evident here will be kindly overlooked.

Still, despite my perspective, I believe that adults of any religion, or of no recognizable religion, will find here deep resonances with their own questions about how to meet death. All that is required is some familiarity with what it means to listen to the heart's questions. After all, isn't it true that when it comes to the human condition, our questions converge, even if our answers diverge?

PROLOG

Matty was born with a single-ventricle heart. Brian and Gina Ventresca adopted him, fully aware that his time with them would be short. But in that poignantly brief span, he bore his illness with remarkably good cheer.

He loved snakes and lizards. He went through a period of wearing ties, as if stealing from an adulthood he would never possess. He welcomed each day as a gift, lacking all presumption that tomorrow was owed him.

During Christmas, 1990, while visiting family and friends in Indianapolis, Matthew suffered pulmonary infection and was put on a respirator. During this time he had a heart catheterization. Shortly after this procedure, Matthew's blood pressure dropped to a critical level. He survived, but his kidneys temporarily stopped functioning. He needed to start dialysis.

Matthew's fluid balance was either too much or too little. There was little margin for error. His heart had a hard time keeping up. For this reason it was unsure if he could survive dialysis, and during the process it appeared he would not. Orders were given to let him die in peace. He had been through enough in his young life.

As the hand of modern medicine pulled back, he stabilized, stopped the spiral downward, and, later that night, improved dramatically. The technique for dialysis was working to keep his fluids balanced, and his health improved significantly. He improved to the point that the doctors decided to take him off the respirator the following day. But that night he suffered a major stroke, leaving him blind, quadriplegic, and minimally responsive. The next two months were spent in the hopes of a recovery, but there was none.

With no hope of any solution in Indiana, his parents flew him by air-ambulance back to California. Matthew was evaluated by his doctors there. It was determined that there was no hope. Two days later the respirator was removed. Matthew was put in his mother's arms, his legs resting on his father. The doctors had thought we would succumb in less than fifteen minutes. He breathed on his own for two and a half hours. God had given this family one last time to be together. Kimy had gone down to the gift shop to get a card for her brother. She wrote in the card, "Dear Matt, I hope you have a nice time in heaven, I love you, Kim." She came into the intensive care unit and gave it to Matt.

Matty died forty days before his ninth birthday. A year after his death, Brian wrote to friends how he, Gina, and their daughter Kimy missed him:

> We miss Matt. We miss the times he would come and sit next to us. We miss the times he would ask us at 3:00 A.M. if he could get into bed with us.
>
> I miss the times he would warm his cold feet on my stomach.
>
> We miss watching him playing with his snake, lizards, and geckos. We miss the times we would fly his kite.
>
> I miss the times I would ride him on my bicycle, with the wind blowing through our hair, holding on for dear life. I miss the times driving on the back roads in the truck with the radio blasting.
>
> We miss the times we watched him playing in the creek with Kimy. We miss the times at Tony's in Marshall, when he and Kimy would throw the oyster shells into the water.
>
> I miss seeing the sculptures in the bathtub he would create for his mom after he took a shower. I miss him helping me build houses with his tool belt wrapped around his waist.
>
> We miss watching the ecstasy on Matt's face when he would discover something new. We miss the times that he was able to go back to school and be with his friends after his hospitalizations. We miss the times sitting next to Matt in the hospital, telling him everything was going to be OK.

We miss the last time we saw Matthew smile. It was before he had the stroke. Kimy walked into the intensive care unit to see him. He looked at her, and this wonderful smile came across his face. We miss Matt's smile.

We miss the times we would read to him in the hospital. We miss Matthew's kisses. We miss the times we would chase after him, tickle him and listen to his laugh. Oh, how we loved his wonderful laugh.

We miss Matthew's hugs. We miss his incredible blue eyes. We miss his long, reddish, blond eyelashes.

We miss going for walks with Matthew, holding his hand. After walking for a while, Matt would want me to carry him. He would always tire out easily, and I would pick him up and carry him on my shoulders.

I miss Matt on my shoulders.

We miss holding our son. We miss Matthew's innocence. We miss Matthew's pure love, the love we had always looked for and finally found.

We miss Matthew. We all miss Matthew.

To Gina, Matthew was an angel sent by God. A messenger of love, a teacher of wonder and curiosity, a model of patience, a crucified and risen Christ.

They picked a lovely spot where they could bury Matty themselves. They had taken care of him since he was seven days old, and they didn't want anyone else to lay his ashes in the ground. On a wooden grave marker, the sketches of fish and snakes are from Matt's artwork, carved by Bill Borras of Inverness, California. It is a beautiful, peaceful place for his final resting. Monarch butterflies cover the ground during migration stopovers, and you can see mountains nestled up to the Pacific Ocean in the distance.

There is much more to say about Matty's life—about his friends, about his hobbies, about all the fond memories he would carry today were he still alive. But that would make a different story and a different book. In this book, I want to think about Matty's story theologically. Theological understanding is not a special technique. All understanding adds insight to experience, and theological understanding adds insights into where we have come from and where we are going. So I will begin from our everyday experiences of life and the many shadows of death that fall upon us. My aim is to put into words our non-verbalized consciousness that we have an origin and a destiny that lie beyond scientific understanding. In particular, I want to reflect on why trying to live a good life is directly connected to our awareness that we will die. And I want to point to ways that we can see the divine, invisible realities that are more important than the merely visible world of our experience.

I will begin, in Chapter 1, by looking at some myths about death. Some of these have numbed us to death's mystery, and so I think it will be helpful to resensitize that area, even at the risk of disturbing the reader. In Chapter 2, I will review some of the major myths from other cultures. Whether or not we agree with these views, they reveal that our own views are just that—views. *Our* myths are built upon life-unto-death experiences that are remarkably similar to the origins of *their* myths. That is, when people of diverse cultures talk about death, their descriptions of raw experience seem to converge. It is when they attempt to interpret those experiences, putting them into stories or some analytical framework that their views diverge.

Then there are the conflicts that occur between mythical views and the voices of modern science, contemporary ethics, and scriptural exegetes. All of these views shape what we might think of Matty's life, so we will attempt to make sense out of apparent contradictions there. So Chapter 3 will be devoted to challenging some of the common beliefs that we have inherited.

From there I want to develop a more positive and consistent view of what Matty Ventresca represents. There is a need to understand death today in terms that are consistent with contemporary science yet go beyond mere physics and psychology. So in Chapter Four I will propose that there is a Law of Caring at work in the universe, and that any salvation of an individual depends on the salvation of that person's community.

A key notion that arises in any discussion of death is "redemption." After all, no one doubts that death is some kind of end, and so the question naturally arises whether the end is total or whether any part of life is redeemed, saved, preserved, lasting. So just as Chapter 4 presents a scientific view of how the world works, Chapter 5 will be devoted to a scientific view of how redemption works when the world's working fails.

In Chapter 6 my reflections become very practical: How to live in death's shadow in our everyday lives, how to make decisions both about small things, and about how we eventually will die. Finally, in

Chapter 7, there will be some closing observations about the eternal importance of human history, about how God reveals truth to us, and about how unique and special each person is in the divine scheme of things.

Throughout these theological reflections, it is important not to get lost in abstractions. So I will frequently appeal either to Matty's experience or your own. Reflections on mortality, after all, are just a thin web of concepts unless they spring from real experience and force a hard look at death in our lives.

CHAPTER 1

The Myths About Death

The metaphors of death,
The myths we learned in school:
Silk dresses neatly tailored,
They emphasize, they fool.

Matty lived too short a life. Yet, we imagine his death as a "passing on." We comfort ourselves with the thought that he may be in a better place. Death is a kind of door, in other words, leading on to the afterlife.

We believe this. The idea of a life after this one seems to be at the very center of our faith. After all, if there is no "better place" than this earthly one, then we could hardly believe in a God who is kind and loving.

On the other hand, there are dangers in this simple view. The idea that death is just a door contains a kind of lie. It suggests a belief about death that is not only untrue but harmful to living. To explain this, let me list three myths about our mortality.

1. The ideal is to live forever.
2. Everyone will experience the death of their bodies as their souls pass on.
3. There is another life coming after this one.

I call these beliefs "myths" in the sense of statements mistakenly held to be true. It is because they are not true that they can distract us from paying the kind of attention to living that we should. Let us look more closely at each one.

MYTH:
THE IDEAL IS TO LIVE FOREVER

The human race has hurled at death every known insult, obstacle, and argument. Death is deaf to them all. Try to negotiate. Cry until your eyes burn dry. Threaten suicide. "Do not go gentle into that good night. Rage, rage against the dying of the light." And when none of that works, try to ignore death. You may succeed for a while, and then death returns—in threes.

Did Gina and Brian and Kimy Ventresca really want Matty to live forever? Never die? Is this the kind of immortality we hope for, a life that does not end in physical death? Of course, no one doubts that we all die. But at the same time many people think of death as meeting their worst fears.

Because we fear death, we presume that we must want to avoid it and, should someone discover a Fountain of Youth, the entire world would break out the champagne. This is the common idea behind "immortality," which, after all, literally means "not dying."

The theologian Karl Rahner, on the other hand, suggested an interesting thought experiment. He described how a Fountain of Youth would actually give us "a miserable sort of freedom." If your life went on without ever ending, you would have a curious type of freedom to be anything you wanted. Be a banker for thirty years. Be an artist for forty years. Be a thief for ten years, spend ten years in prison once they catch you, and then get out and be a cop for ten years. Be married to this person for forty years, then to that person for sixty years. Move stop move stop move stop move stop.

What are you then? You are nothing at all. You are connected to no one in particular because eventually you will have gotten hooked and unhooked to millions of people. After thousands and thousands of years, no one would be unique because everyone would have done practically everything. All identity would be temporary. People wouldn't bother keeping their names. You wouldn't know whom you were meeting at a cocktail party and, in any case, probably wouldn't care. Your circle of friends, your nationality, your religious community would have no value except in the short term.

It wouldn't even make sense to try to be a good person. People would praise the good we do and blame us for evil, but all the good and evil taken together would have no final bearing on whether we lived a good life or not. After all, if adults today eventually forget the stupid or selfish things they did as children, how much more "forgetful" would we be in a life that went on without end? The past would simply have no meaning for who we are at any present moment.

We may not notice it, but this jaundiced view of unending life lurks in everyone. If this skepticism weren't there, if we thought instead that what we choose to do today can be completely undone in some tomorrow, then we wouldn't agonize over our choices. We'd probably just flip coins. Our decisions literally would not mean anything.

But we expect that what we do now has some meaning to it. The key here is the idea of meaning.

The realm of meaning is very real. It may not be geographical; you can't travel there. Nor is it any narrow period of time; you can't take a "time out" from meaningful living. This is the realm, I believe, that ancient religions spoke of when they spoke of immortality. For example, the highest achievement of the person in Hindu belief is to realize that immortality lies in the meaning of one's life, not in its duration, nor in experiences that we imagine must come after life. Hindu sacred writings (the Katha Upanishad and the Bhagavad Gita) describe a liberation from successive reincarnations. The Hindu who does not yet realize the illusory status of death will, after dying, eventually return—for another try as it were. But the Hindu who realizes that there is always divine guidance at one's side (in the person of Krishna) surrenders all fear about death. One discovers one's true self (the Atman) by a leap of faith that death is not the enemy. Then one is fully united with Brahman and is freed from the burden of incessant returns to earth. What is important here is not the literal descriptions of reincarnations, nor what may be the actual names of divine advocates. What counts is action, not words or ideas. The saving action is to surrender our dread about death and trust that we will be guided by powers higher than our own. Guided toward meaningfulness.

When we look at people across the globe, we see that people everywhere hope that the meaning of their lives is not arbitrary or temporary. No matter of what religion, no matter if no religion, no matter how educated in speaking of spiritual reality, men and women everywhere hope that life carries meaning that death cannot abolish.

What are we thinking about when we say that we want meaning in our lives? For some, it is simply a matter of impressing others, being "meaningful" to them, as if meaning and fame are the same thing. But to people who know that audiences are fickle and fame is brief, leading a meaningful life depends on what takes place in the heart, not what public opinion may be. To act with meaning includes taking responsibility. It involves making commitments. It means following through on one's ideas and promises. Having meaning in our lives bears the same sense as when we say, "I mean it!" or "I mean to make some changes around here." That is, the only way to find meaning in life is to make a difference—an improvement, we hope—in the life we share with others.

The same idea can be expressed in terms of freedom. When it comes to leading a meaningful life, there is universal agreement that some measure of freedom is necessary. But too often people think of freedom strictly as the absence of external barriers to doing what we'd like. For example, no restrictions on free speech, on worship, on political and economic rights. But there are millions of people who enjoy these freedoms who still lead lives without meaning. The reason is that they are not free *inside*. They experience internal barriers to finding meaning in their lives. So full freedom must include the absence of internal barriers to acting in a meaningful way. But if meaningful action involves taking responsibility for one's life, then freedom may be defined as the ability to be responsible. The people who are truly free not only live in countries where rights are protected, they live *in themselves* as responsible for the choices they make.

If true freedom involves taking responsibility, however, true responsibility is not possible, Rahner says, without death. Just how death is necessary for true freedom may become clear if we compare how children think about freedom to how their parents think about it. Parents usually have to impress on their children that you have to balance freedom with responsibility. "You can't just play all day; you've got to do the chores." In other words, freedom is just the free time left over when duties are done. Parents don't treat themselves that way, however. Mature adults do not divide their time between freedom and responsibility. Somewhere in early adulthood, they realized that to really be somebody, you've got to take charge of your life. To take that charge, it is necessary to struggle against inner compulsions as well as against the expectations of others. Being "free" comes to mean not just freedom from chores but, more importantly, freedom to become what you want to be. If you want to be free from compulsions, if you want to avoid roles that are not consistent with what you want out of life, you have to take responsibility. That kind of freedom is not "balanced" by responsibility; it is the same thing as responsibility.

Death is the tutor here because it is death that first raises the question, "What will I be?" Death is necessary for true freedom because, without it, we would not be serious about defining the selves we hope to become. Without death, the very question of the meaning of our lives would never come up. Death may stand at the far end of our lives, but it casts a long shadow. Death is present in every moment of our lives calling out, again and again, "What will you be?"

So, if we can ignore for a moment the fact that dying is usually painful, death itself is not the enemy of life. Since we cannot have an identity otherwise, death is part of each person's uniqueness. That is, what makes each of us the special, irreplaceable person that we are becoming is our common destiny in the grave. What is more, since it is our uniqueness, our peculiarity, our individuality that invites others to love us, then death also makes us lovable. After all, isn't it true that what we love in our friends is the way they deal with life? We love how they work and how they relax. We love them not as rigid statuaries but as revolutionaries of the spirit, fighting to build up an identity. Without realizing it, in most cases, it is death that forces them to open themselves up to us. And us to them.

The kind of immortality that we want, then, is not unending life. If we are correct in saying that death has a role to play in making us lovable to one another, then we can get an insight into why God may have included death in our destiny in the first place. That is, if death is what makes mutual love possible, then death appears to be God's idea for our singularity as individuals and our solidarity as a community. Death forces us to make something of ourselves and, having made something of ourselves, we make it possible to be loved by others and thereby weave us into the rich fabric of a community. Indeed, we naturally seek to put our stamp on our surroundings and to be loved by others. Death is love's mentor, reminder, and incentive. And love is death's purpose, reason, and result. Here, in creativity and love, not mere unendingness, we find the "immortality" we crave.

When someone we love dies, this subtler dimension of immortality seizes our consciousness. Is there really much consolation in the thought that he or she has migrated to a better place? True, for those who suffered at life's end, we may be happy their suffering is over. But the deeper consolation comes from every good word that came from their mouths, every genuine engagement, every kind deed. We discount whether or not their contributions were to our benefit; we focus instead on the deeper judgment that their contributions were good of themselves.

The upshot is that when we feel the jitters about our deaths, we should transpose the object of those jitters. Rather we should feel uneasy about being unreal, fake, oblivious, or self-centered. Real immortality lies in the deathless character of taking responsibility for our lives.

These ideas about the real meaning of an "immortal" life are not foreign to Christian scriptures. John the Evangelist reports Jesus as talking about "life eternal." There, the Greek word for eternal is *aionion*, which basically means deep, not long. It means an incredibly rich life, not an incredibly lengthy one. Even the English word, "eternal" comes from the Latin, meaning "not temporal" or "not in the temporal order." That's all. It does not mean going on forever. That meaning, doubtless influenced by misplaced hopes in unending life, would still be "temporal" in the sense of "in time." "Eternal" means almost the opposite. It means not about time at all.

John also uses the term "from above" to talk about the same thing. He realized that eternal life is far better represented by a vertical arrow lifting earthly concerns to divine significance than by a horizontal arrow stretching on to infinity in time. Again, in the story of Lazarus we can see this vertical quality of eternal life. Lazarus' sister Martha said to Jesus, "I know that my brother will be raised up on the last day." And Jesus answered her, "I am the raising up." He seemed to be saying that salvation is now, not at the end of life. Perfectionist that she was, Martha was distracted by the future, as if the end is all that really counts. Jesus snaps her out of her spiritual coma by alerting her to the presence of the non-temporal (the eternal) in life at the present moment. For the rest of her born days, she will remember this one as the day she embraced immortality.

For the Ventresca's too. They remember a day when they flew a kite with Matty; they cherish a memory of a cherubic Matty with a snake around his neck. The beauty, the meaning, of Matty's life flashed out in revelation. True, they mourn his early death. But mixed in with that mourning, inseparable from it in anyone who mourns, is the poignant joy over a moment of shared transcendence.

MYTH:
THERE IS ANOTHER LIFE COMING AFTER THIS ONE

To our children we keep it simple: After you die, you go through a kind of door to a new life, a different life. If you're good, you go to a better life, a life with God. Matty's sister Kimy wished him a good time in heaven.

Even to adults we keep it simple: We are but pilgrims. Our lives are "transitory," meaning that we are just in transit, on our way somewhere else. When we sing "Swing low, sweet chariot, comin' for to carry me home," we remind ourselves that we are not home yet; coming to our real home happens later. Many adults avoid saying "died" as if it were obscene. Recently, in front of the kids, they have more easily broken the taboos on "my period," and "penis." Rather than "died," they still prefer "passed on."

It is important to note, however, that in the long history of humankind, talk about "passing on" is a novelty. Belief in a life following this is rather new. The majority of people who ever lived gave it no thought. Even among those who consider themselves religious, we find many for whom the idea of an afterlife has absolutely no bearing on how they live. Confucius taught a high morality side-by-side with a skepticism about a life following this one. The Mesopotamian Epic of Gilgamesh (7th century B.C.) praises civic virtue and the raising of children as the only possible meaning of "immortality."

It comes as a shock to many Christians to learn that there is scarcely a hint of an afterlife in the Hebrew Bible. Why in the world would anyone want to be good if there were no payoff in a next life? For what reason would a Jew be faithful to God and the Commandments if there were no hope of ever seeing God, being with God? The Book of Deuteronomy portrays God as loving and kind, yet no one seems to have entertained the idea that God would—even could—share divine life with a human after death. Apparently it wasn't until about 200 years before Christ, when Greek and Egyptian merchants passed through the Holy Land and shared philosophical ideas about immortality, that the general population of Israelites first considered that death may not be the end.

Are we now enlightened or are we in a deeper darkness about life after we die? Does this simple view of passing on to another land do justice to the spiritual insights of forebears who lived without this view? Frankly, I find it refreshing to be skeptical about an afterlife. The idea of an afterlife can rob death of its power and meaning. It tends to depict death as just a check valve through which people squirt into another, happier chamber.

Also, when we combine the idea of an afterlife with a forgiving God, we give moral laziness more allowance than it deserves. If we believe that we really continue after dying, especially if we're convinced that a forgiving God will somehow erase even our mistakes, then there's no big urgency to make something of ourselves. Morality loses its urgency. Why the big fuss about this world if it passes away anyway?

No doubt, many people who imagine death as just a passage to the "next" world live without much fear of death. But isn't this the same as saying they also live without much fear of "not living"? Might they be just drifting through life without paying much attention to the voices of the heart? Isn't this just a deceptive combination of luck and stupidity? Have they never experienced the fear of having lived a shallow, ignorant, silly life? Wouldn't they be better off to have seriously doubted that there is a life after this one? There would certainly be a lot less nonsense about this life if they had.

One unnoticed but terribly damaging aspect of the afterlife myth is its individualism. It portrays God as snatching us one-by-one out of this world and hauling us into the next. "You can't take it with you" means that nothing of this world goes with you. All God is really interested in is individuals. True, many expect to meet again all those who went before them. But we imagine such a meeting in pure white abstraction from the palpable details of the life we shared together. To hell with the impatiens you and your spouse planted in the front yard. The time you spent helping a friend put in a fence is "just history." The human environment is merely an envelope used for the delivery of our souls, which are deemed the part that is "really us." Human history is really just a string of events that we list in our minds; there really is nothing going forward for us as a group that concerns God. For those who rely on this individualistic myth to dream about heaven, human concern for this world is often little more than a hobby.

We tend to forget how ignorant we are about an afterlife. We have no reliable data that life really goes on after dying. We have beliefs, of course, but that is the problem: many of our beliefs make such trumpery of human joy and happiness that they effectively deny what is staring us in the face—that when people die, their minds collapse, their hearts chill, and their bodies decompose.

One way to avoid looking at how completely the human person dies is to suggest, as Socrates did, that our spiritual part goes on while our physical part dies. People have even claimed to have seen a dead person's "soul" rising up to heaven. These may be comforting notions, but, again, we have no way of verifying in our experience that humans are so constituted that a soul can slough off a body like this. It is still only a hypothesis that we have a "soul" or a disembodied "spirit." In common, non-philosophical usage, the words "soul" and "spirit" refer to the ability of a person to be present to surroundings, to have impact on others, to be a fully engaging human being. For example, "Ella Fitzgerald really has soul!" "The Tigers have lost their spirit." This kind of soul and spirit are powers, not objects. It is these powers that really die when our bodies give out. It is this kind of loss that makes death so hard to bear, as we lose our sense of humor, our memories, and our power to care.

What kind of God is this that makes it necessary for us to tell children about a life following this one, only to be disturbed as adults about its sorry implications? Why would God give us an imagination to picture a next life in vivid detail and then lead us to realize that life with God may not be "next" in an uninterrupted stream of experience?

It may well be a matter of good teaching practice in which we oversimplify things for beginners. After all, life for those who have died is supposed to be utterly beyond our powers of description. The Apostle Paul commented that the sufferings of this life are nothing compared to the glory of life with God—indeed, these present sufferings train us to bear the weight of that glory. Unfortunately, this kind of talk does not get very far with the kids. They want something recognizable. So we talk in rich, palpable terms about heaven "up there" in a life "after this." Eventually, when children have come to understand something of the mystery of life, they also are able to see the difference between simply affirming in faith that there is a life beyond this one and trying to describe what it looks like when you get there. The bare affirmation that there is life "beyond" this one is what ultimately holds firm while the descriptions shift and fade.

So, as we get older, trust deepens. We see that the paintings of heaven and of God are quite unlike the paintings of, say, George Washington. Paintings of heaven point to a mystery far different than the painted image, while paintings of Washington are supposed to be close approximations. Because our descriptions of life with God are just symbolic of a reality that cannot be put into clear words, many people go through a period of years without the religious symbols, or of paying them no attention.

Eventually, though, as hope continues its relentless rising, some of the disenchanted return to these inadequate pointers to God. They talk of angels again, and they let the church architecture lift their spirits heavenward. They dote on the baby Jesus in the crib. They talk about Adam and Eve with a seriousness that rivals the critical historian's. They imagine their personal history as on a one-way track from birth, through dying, to an afterlife. It has become obvious to them that these poor images are the best we can muster, and we need something to help us focus our hope in the face of agonies unimaginable to youngsters. For many, the very fact that we have to tell simple stories is a humbling admission that God had always been this close.

This return to the naïve descriptions marks a major step in the spiritual development of adults. The intelligence of a child differs from that of an adult not only in the amount of knowledge. It differs in the ability to pursue questions about how things work, about whether beliefs are true, about what may be truly good. But not all these questions find answers. Some things remain mysterious even to mature adults, and so they return to the simplistic pictures. But there's a difference. In the child, the pictures stand for reality, and where there is no picture there can be no reality. In the adult who has discovered such unpicturable realities as a language, a culture, a mind, a commitment, a promise, or a threat, there is also the discovery that some unpicturable realities can never be fully understood. They will remain a mystery.

The philosopher Paul Ricoeur calls this return to the simple pictures a "second naiveté." Their childhood belief in the details had to give way to their developing intelligences. The symbols had to be broken. And at this point, many teens and young adults were unable to see the difference between a bare affirmation of something beyond and a long, luxuriant description of what that something might be. They felt as though they had lost their faith in God, when they only lost their faith in our powers of description to get a handle on mystery. In the meantime, life continues to force a person to deal with authentic living and to experience a deepening need for help in being fair, understanding, and caring. The desire for ever fuller life often turns a person toward God in the dark, without the thin representations of words and pictures. Here is where the adult decision is made about God. Here is where real religious confirmation happens. And once a person realizes that God is all that everything in us ultimately seeks—whatever that may be—then he or she returns to the simple symbols and stories with a smile and a deep trust that they work.

Death may not be a door. The afterlife may not be next. But despite these disturbing realizations, there is no reason people cannot pray, "Kind God, we trust that these, our primitive images, really bring us to you as you really are." There is no reason Kimy can't wish Matty well in heaven. There is no reason we can't believe *that* God's care will never end, even though we cannot imagine *how*.

MYTH:
EVERYONE WILL EXPERIENCE THE DEATH OF THEIR BODIES AS THEIR SOULS PASS ON

On the contrary. No one has ever experienced death.

Even though everyone dies, the moment of death is nothing anyone ever experiences as it occurs. You cannot watch yourself die any more than you can watch yourself fall asleep.

This is because dying is the death of experiencing. We say, "You lose consciousness." But at the point where living ends, there is no more live "you" to lose anything. The "you" that has governed the multileveled organism of your body and mind and heart has died. Matty Ventresca was in and out of consciousness for two full months before he died. To him, the last losing of consciousness was no different than the one before.

The fabled "moment of death" is far less dramatic and far more mundane than most of us believe. Some writers have rhapsodized about this moment. But there is no "moment" of death, at least not in the sense of any other moment that came before it. When I experience a moment of silence, a moment of reflection, or a moment of discouragement, these are brief spells. They pass; something else comes next. At death, however, there is nothing "next" for the dead person. I am not saying there is nothing "left." Nor am I saying everything about the person has vanished. Nor that at death, as some suicide advocates say, "You just rot." I only mean to point out that the so-called "moment" of death is the end of moment-filled life altogether.

People with "near death" experiences tell of having their entire lives pass before their eyes in an instant. Some talk of walking in a dark tunnel toward an alluring light. But these dream-like accounts are relatively rare (and quite recent in history). Most people with near-death experiences have nothing to say, except that they lost consciousness. The long-standing and majority experience of being near death is like falling asleep. Consciousness fades. In some cases dreams begin, and some of those dreams (influenced by expectation perhaps) may include compacted visions of one's life or the feeling of walking toward some light. In other, more rare cases, medical teams seem to bring a cadaver "back to life." This gives tabloids a rich lode for mining. However, the revived person has never been "dead" very long, and the doctors bring up the case more to challenge the medical definition of "dead" than to give evidence of a next life.

The conclusion staring at us here is that if human knowledge depends on how we interpret experience, then our reliable knowledge of the experience of death is zero. Some people will point to great literature on death without bothering to ask whether fiction can convey the kind of information we want. Much of it aims to reassure us and comfort us in the face of the frightful unknown, not to predict a certain chain of experiences that everyone will undergo. Others will point to revered philosophers whose teachings they accept as a whole without screening out uncertain parts. But by what means these sages arrived at their knowledge, if not either through understanding experience or believing others who understood their experience? Since none of us is exempt from the requirement that human knowledge is derived from experience and should make sense of experience, then no one holds a privileged position for understanding death.

Although I believe this logic is sound, logic seldom convinces. Many will cling to a belief that they "walk on" in some sense. They may take their stand on a faith that if they "die," they are reincarnated to live yet another life. Usually they rely on a mental pictures. The imagine a "soul" tucked inside a body. Ask them to explain this and they usually describe a wispy, ethereal being that is not truly spiritual in the sense of being unbound by space and time; it is only a spooky version of a body that is invisible to the naked eye. This soul must travel upwards to heaven or downwards to Hades. It must mark time waiting for God's judgment or for a subsequent reincarnation. To my mind, this "soul" is as physical as that old radio character, The Shadow. You cannot see him, but he is there, then; or here, now. This invisible-but-physical soul has no legitimate claim to the rich legacy of philosophic ideas proposed by the likes of Plato and Aristotle.

Still, we can be sympathetic to these views. After all, most afterlife theories that describe a soul wandering further on a journey, whether straight up to bliss, straight down to damnation, or around for another trying spell on earth, originated long before any human being was capable of distinguishing between a symbolic account and a proposition. A symbolic account describes. It paints a vivid picture that brings together in compact fashion a host of analogies about life's mystery. The purpose of symbols is to bestow certain values and feelings on the transforming experiences of life—birth, company, sex, fighting, bad weather, forgiveness, revenge, good fortune, suffering, and death. About death, the preferred symbol is a journey because it represents a mixture of good fortune and bad succeeding each other over time, and each turn partially determining our final destination.

In contrast, a proposition states a truth without ambiguity. It states what is so and avoids descriptions or explanations of *how* that truth can be so. The essential proposition about death that most people make is, simply, "death is not final" or "in death all is not lost." Just *how* death is not final and *how* all is not lost are different questions, questions we still cannot answer.

With this distinction between a symbolic account and a proposition in mind, we can more easily understand the classical philosophic view of what a "soul" really is. The classical view is a proposition, not a symbolic account of some invisible body. When we say we have souls, we are simply saying that there are principles in us that give power to our living—the source of this man's wondering and loving, of that woman's curiosity and wit. We are simply saying that there is a nonphysical source in each person of his or her ability to think and feel. There is no warrant for presuming that these principles, or powers, can shed the material body and live on their own. No one found a soul during a surgery on a body. This spiritual power occupies no space in us, no more than the Law of Gravity occupies space in every apple. No, we concluded the existence of the "soul" from noticing that people can act intelligently and responsibly. Moreover, there is overwhelming evidence that our physical makeup and spiritual principles shape each other as we grow up. In other words, as long as our bodies are alive, so are the powers that make us human—our "souls." But when our bodies give out and our minds and hearts no longer function, then what we called our "souls" has vanished.

I press the point because of the danger of imagining a soul that can escape the body. It makes it too easy to excuse ourselves from making a total act of faith. We can think of our souls as "naturally" made for an afterlife, rather than just as subject to death as our bodies. Our faith becomes limited to hoping that God will be kind to us when we come up yonder. We can forget how fragile is our belief that death is not an end. That belief itself requires an act of faith. If we accept that the whole "I" that we are to ourselves truly dies, then we are more likely to live in an unsettling faith in God. We are likely to remember how absolute is our dependence on God's free choice not to abandon us in death. After all, just as we did not have to be born into this life, so no rule binds God to retain anything beyond our deaths.

I do not feel disloyal to my Christian tradition if I note that many Christians deny the awful completeness of death. Certainly, it is appropriate that Christians would see humankind as represented in Christ, so that Christ represents what is finest about human nature, including the continuous struggle to live authentically. But, in various ways people often transfer onto humanity a misguided view of the resurrection of Christ. Some believe that Jesus "came back to life." Or they hold that Jesus used his miraculous powers to "get up again." They may say Jesus died, but they imagine that Jesus "continued," consciously experiencing being laid in a tomb and, on the following Sunday, getting up much as you and I wake up in the morning. They project onto Jesus what they hope about their own deaths, namely, that you really just fall asleep and wake up on the other side—all part of a natural process.

A closer reading of the New Testament, however, gives a much more disturbing picture. The fate of Jesus is dominated by God's terrifying freedom. The evangelists go to some lengths to point out that Jesus really died as completely as we all do. His "resurrection" is presented as nothing at all like the raising of Lazarus. Jesus did not raise himself as he raised the son of the widow of Naim. The scriptures here presume that her son and Lazarus will eventually die for good, but that the resurrected life of Jesus is no longer subject to death. The point is that the resurrection is not a miracle performed by Jesus. It is not intended to be proof of Jesus' divine status. It is not a cure for Jesus' death. Much of the earliest preaching used the formula, "Jesus lives," and almost every New Testament texts about a raising do not say "Jesus rose;" they say "Jesus was raised." In other words, the resurrection proclaimed in the Gospels is not the work of Jesus getting up from death. It is God's free work "raising" Jesus after death. The first disciples of Jesus believed that God raised him to a level of life beyond death. To my reading of these passages, the common belief that resurrection after death is natural to us represents more a faith in a natural process than in God. It relies on a guaranteed movement going from birth to death to resurrection rather than on God's free and loving choice to bestow a resurrected life on the dead. As far as we can tell from direct experience, there is only birth and death. Nothing before and nothing after.

There is more. In the view of Christians of New Testament times, if Jesus did not "come back" to life, neither did he return to a "divine" life that replaced his human life. That is, he did not shed his humanity. They believed that if the human life of Jesus really means anything, then God preserves what it means. (Recall what we said earlier about how immortality is essentially about meaning, not about duration.) God always lived in Jesus during his earthly lifetime, no less than in the centuries following his death. God removed Jesus from a mode of living that the living experience, but it is very important for Christians to believe that Jesus continues to live an entirely human life—despite our ignorance of what the "human life" of the dead might mean. The reasoning here is that Jesus remains eternally human. If he somehow sloughed his humanity, then his resurrection would be no pledge about human destiny at all. God would just be showing off. But if Jesus retains his humanity, then that truth becomes the good news for humanity that God preserves everything that is truly human.

Christians do well to recognize that scriptures depict Jesus as completely dependent on God, with no power of his own to beat death. They might recall how Jesus cried out in genuine desperation, "Father, why have you forsaken me?" And the Father answered . . . well, the Father didn't answer anything. There were—and still are—no explanations forthcoming, either from God or philosophy, why we are completely forsaken in death. Whether or not one is Christian, the cry of Jesus is a plea we will all cry out as we face our own deaths: "Why have you forsaken us?" Death takes absolutely everything from us. God will seem callous to human pain. God will not snatch us from the grief and emotional agony of losing those we love. God will not spare us from the cruel vocation of departing from dear friends as we come to our own deaths absolutely alone.

Only by looking at death in this way can we see how deep—and how simple—our faith must be. The naked act of faith is the act of realizing that something is true despite our lack of understanding, of confidence, or of any clear image of what death means. Certainly, it helps to understand death—its psychological and medical aspects. It helps to feel strong and confident in the face of death. It helps to carry a vivid image of walking on into the hands of God. But these supports given by understanding, by feelings, and by imagination are not always there when we need them. Our faith must stand strong whether or not we feel comforted by symbolic accounts about walking on from this life into the next. We count ourselves lucky if we enjoy some insight and emotional support in that extremity, and even if we do, we know that, compared to faith, our understanding, feelings, and imagination are rubber crutches.

Let me be precise about this. It helps immensely to locate in ourselves just which of our many faculties is the most important when it comes to faith. Of all the faculties we rely on for living day to day—feelings, intelligence, imagination, and judgments—only judgments can be an act of faith. While it is often enriched by the other faculties, when it acts by itself, it is cool and lean and hungry.

Faith confronts death by the simple but radical judgment that death is not the enemy. Faith sees through the vacuous threats posed by death; faith judges that nothing of value in our lives will be lost. Faith rests in the simple assurance that God loves each person now and will not let any person be utterly abolished.

It doesn't take a Christian to realize that one's faith has no more and no less security than the faith of Jesus. One does not have to subscribe to any formal creeds of the Christian churches to believe that we will be raised (whatever that means) to intimate life with God. Believers of all stripes bear the hope that whatever "happened" to

Jesus after his crucifixion might possibly happen to us, despite our radical and enduring ignorance of what that happening might be. But hope, we should remember, is a desire rendered confident by faith, not by any assurance that we will walk through some bright door of cloud and skirt the horrendous totality of death.

What did Matty experience? He experienced the same falling unconsciousness that he experienced every night and at every nap. No more. And no less, either, since we cannot overlook his deep faith in God. Even though his faith was supported by vivid imaginations and stories about life with God, he lived and died with a truth embraced—an acknowledgment that God will not let anything good vanish. He allowed his life to slip away without protesting any unfairness. How could it be unfair if death is not his enemy? It seems more honest and sobering to believe that he did not watch himself die through some sort of worried spiritual eyes but rather that he felt no need to watch out for death at all.

Just as the Ventrescas watched Matty's spirit wane, so they watched his spirit die. If there is any hope, any ultimate destiny, any fulfillment of the reason we were created, then it lies in a complete surrender of our entire selves. It lies in a transformation of our selves by One whom we cannot control and whose arrival comes as pure gift.

CHAPTER 2
Our Many Voices

*Who knows the heart of Death—
Arjuna, Buddha, Job?
Maybe the widow next door
in her curlers and flannel robe.*

CONTEMPLATING DEATH

The previous chapter aimed to be upsetting. We wanted to debunk some myths about death, not to deny them all significance, but rather to shake our complacency about their true meaning. The present chapter aims to be equally upsetting.

We can sharpen our sense of the mystery of our mortality by looking at classical texts about death. By listening to other voices, we will realize that other people put surprisingly different interpretations on death-related experiences than we do. Plus we gain a certain intellectual distance from the ideas we grew up with. Not that we abandon our traditions. On the contrary, we realize that *our* ideas about death are symbolic accounts and not philosophical explanations. We realize that other symbolic accounts were created by people with anxieties about death remarkably similar to ours—a realization which ought to leave our hearts in deeper awe. This is a far better way of being faithful to our tradition because we will more likely understand the depth and nuances of the experiences of the people who wrote our traditional texts. Without that understanding, we run the danger of interpreting these documents in ways their authors never meant.

First, a caution. Classical texts are exclusively narrative or didactic. They do not distinguish propositional truth from the embellishments of a story and the practicalities of instruction. The stories of creation in *Genesis* describe God creating the world in a week, creating the first couple, discovering that couple's disobedience, and driving them out of paradise. What kind of truth are we supposed to realize here? Fundamentalists will insist that the only kind of truth is what is imagined—that it took seven days, that there was first a man, then a woman, etc. Theologians and literary critics read this very differently. They take *Genesis* as a symbolic narrative, at the core of which there are a few profound propositional truths. We might state these core truths in propositional form as follows:

1. God did the creating;
2. sex is good; and
3. God is not responsible for sin in the world.

The classic texts of other religions are usually symbolic narratives as well and, like *Genesis*, contain a few core truths that point to the main realities in which we put our faith.

We need to be careful, therefore. How should we read these classics without either reducing them to mere fiction or inflating them to eyewitness accounts? How can we distinguish between essential beliefs and nonessential dressing? It all depends on the kind of questions we're asking. For example, here are some of the essential questions that classical texts address:

- Is death the end of me?
- Is there a God who cares for me?
- Is the human race involved in realities of a higher order?
- Do my everyday decisions make any ultimate difference?

Notice how these questions deal with what death means to me personally. The answers to these questions should make a difference to my everyday living. People will answer either a Yes or a No to each of these. They answer neither with a description of events, nor with a scientific explanation of any process. The answer is a simple assent to what is true. Saying it's a simple assent, however, does not mean that the answer is easy to give. The answer people give shapes how they live. People who change their answers have undergone a conversion. From that point on they will live in a different world.

To give a contrasting example, here are some non-essential questions:

- How long ago did the world begin?
- What will it feel like after I die?
- Is God going to bring everyone to Heaven?
- Is it OK to forgo artificial life support if I ever fall into a permanently vegetative state?

These questions deal only remotely with death's meaning for me personally. The answers won't make much difference to how I live. These are matters of opinion, not conversion. The answers give a description or advice, not a truth about the world we live in.

It is not easy to keep our focus on the essential questions. Much of what we read in a given day has no real significance for how live. We have become accustomed to reading just for familiarity. Reading for familiarity can be complicated, but it is not demanding. In half an hour, you can recognize in the pages below the general tone and beliefs of some of history's major religious and secular groups. You may be able to describe to others what you read here. You may even find some of the narratives particularly touching, either for the beauty of the prose or transparency of their authors' anguished quests.

By contrast, focusing on the essential questions is actually simpler, but more demanding and far more rewarding. It involves asking yourself whether or not the beliefs held by others in response to the essential questions about life are *true*. The answer you give is not just a concept; it involves a commitment. It means deciding for yourself whether you would allow your eventual death to change the way you live. It means prioritizing your concerns for friendship, wealth, health, and fame in the same way that the classical texts did for the people who revered them.

We easily become accustomed to our unanswered, essential questions. We forget how important certain questions are to our daily life. Classical texts are not the strange beliefs of foreigners; they are expressions of concerns you and everyone else wonders about often. So I recommend that you read the texts with an ear bent to hear the propositional truth at their core.

Even young Matty Ventresca believed that life is larger than we can directly experience. His universe extended beyond what we can touch and name. And in this kindly place, he felt secure. In his way he echoed a belief expressed by Dame Julian of Norwich: "All shall be well . . . You yourself shall see that all manner of thing shall be well."

"All shall be well." A simple proposition. In a calm assent of the contemplative part of his mind, Matty acknowledged this to be so.

So let yourself feel the bewilderment, the search, and then—as far as possible—the discovery about the kind of faith that meets death well. More often than not, these questions have *not* been adequately answered by your religion or personal philosophy. Even if you disagree with the truths held by others, or prioritize human needs differently, I believe that you will find that their *questions* about death resonate with questions in your own heart.

THE EPIC OF GILGAMESH

The Epic of Gilgamesh is one of the oldest texts on death. The selection below was finalized in the 7th century, B.C., but it contains elements extending as far back as 2,000 B.C. You will find that it appeals to anyone's love of a good story, but also that it says a lot about what it means to be a human.

Gilgamesh, who was half god, loved Endiku, who was half animal, and through their friendship they plumbed the depths of being fully human. Endiku and Gilgamesh first befriended each other through their respect for each other's strength in killing monsters. It so happened that Gilgamesh had attracted the interest of the goddess Ishtar, but when she offered to sleep with him, he rejected her. When Endiku is wounded after he and Gilgamesh have beheaded the giant Humbaba, Ishtar makes Endiku's wound fatal because she wants to get even with Gilgamesh for rejecting her sexual advances.

Enkidu tells Gilgamesh his fears of dying, but Gilgamesh chides him for fearing what happens to everyone anyway. When Endiku finally dies, however, Gilgamesh feels the full brunt of mortality as he mourns his lost friend. The awesome nature of death comes home to him not because of his own eventual death but because death has stripped him of someone he loved. Mortally wounded in his soul, he travels afar, searching for the meaning of death. The selection ends with the counsel of a common barmaid to Gilgamesh, telling him that death cannot be avoided. All we can do is relish the pleasant times and rejoice in our children.

Like most epic narratives, Gilgamesh can be read as an allegory of the human condition. Here, Gilgamesh represents our spiritual selves coming to terms with Enkidu, our animal selves. Notice the interplay of how spiritual and bodily powers intermingle and shape each other. At first they befriend each other. Yet when death approaches, they begin to part. Here's the story:

> Gilgamesh was king of Uruk, a city set between the Tigris and Euphrates rivers in ancient Babylon. Enkidu was born on the Steppe, where he grew up among the animals. Gilgamesh was called a god and a human; Enkidu was an animal and a human. This is the story of their becoming human together.

> "Why are you worried about death? Only the gods are immortal anyway," sighed Gilgamesh. "What humans do is nothing, so fear is never justified. What happened to your power that once could challenge and equal mine? I will go ahead of you, and if I die, I will at least have the reward of having people say: He died in war against Humbaba. You cannot discourage me with fears and hesitations."

Gilgamesh and Enkidu proceed to kill Humbaba, but Enkidu is wounded. Ishtar makes advances to Gilgamesh, but he rejects her. So she causes Enkidu's wound to be mortal, which Enkidu learns in a dream.

He (Enkidu) looked at Gilgamesh and said: "You will be left alone, unable to understand in a world where nothing lives anymore as you thought it did. Nothing like yourself, everything like dead clay before the river makes the plants burst out along its beds, dead and . . ." He became bitter in his tone again: "Because of *her* [Ishtar]. She made me see things with human eyes, and human eyes see death in things. That is what it is to be a human. You'll know when you have lost the strength to see the way you once did. You'll be alone and wander, looking for that life that's gone or some eternal life you have to find. . . . My pain is that my eyes and ears no longer see and hear the same as yours do. Your eyes have changed. You are crying. You never cried before. It's not like you. Why am I to die, you to wander on alone? Is that the way it is with friends?"

Gilgamesh sat hushed as his friend's eyes stilled. In his silence he reached out to touch the friend whom he had lost.

[After Enkidu dies, Gilgamesh sets out on a journey to visit Utnapishtim, a man who was given everlasting life. That visit will prove to be fruitless, but on his way, Gilgamesh is encouraged to give up his search for everlasting life by Siduru, a barmaid.]

"You will never find an end to grief by going on," she said to the one half-sleeping at her side, leaning forward to wipe the perspiration from his face. Although his eyes were open, his whole self felt asleep far off alone in some deep forest planted in his flesh, through which he felt his way in pain without the help of friends. She spoke as to a child who could not understand all the futility that lay ahead, yet who she knew should go on to repeat, repeat, repeat the things men had to learn. "The gods gave death to humans and kept life for themselves. That is the only way it is. Cherish your rests; the children you might have. You are a thing that carries so much tiredness."

There is much wisdom in this symbolic narrative. In the human journey, the daring aspirations of the spirit are continually tethered by the earth-bound duties of the body. Among youth especially, and among youth who enjoy the benefits of civilization, the spirit believes it is immortal. Not that the mind disbelieves death—there simply is no need to fear death. Youthful optimism is rooted in personal success, not in concern for one's progeny. Such is the view of young half-god Gilgamesh.

Enkidu comes from hard country. Half-animal, he knows the smell of blood and carcass; he wisely fears deep water and dark forest. His world is populated with beasts and warlocks. Laws, schools, and grammar are just the odd preoccupations of urban dwellers. Still, he is persuaded by spirit to take a risk, and he pays dearly.

As we age, we discover that our bodies cannot support our spirits' ambitions. Our bodies issue their warnings that time is running out: We start limping and aching and propping ourselves up with various crutches. Eventually the spirit realizes an awful truth: it had presumed an immortality that is not possible apart from our bodies. Spirit, in fact, dies its own death. Wherever spirit has come to love the body, to cherish it, to respect it, to luxuriate in its pleasures and protect it from harm, the very depth of that friendship binds the spirit to mortality and destines it for its own pain and death.

The lesson summary is delivered by the plainest folk. It is a barmaid, not a guru, who has the final wisdom. She tells Gilgamesh that his death and pain were inevitable from the beginning. Get used to it. In the meantime, savor the good times you have, and be glad that you leave children—the only claim on immortality there is.

The epic may not tell us much about faith, but it does raise at least one question that any faith capable of meeting death must answer. Can my faith accept the fact that my spirit really dies? I have disturbing evidence from how I deal with sickness that I lack such a faith: sickness makes me depressed; my spirit sinks and I hate it. Is it possible to have a faith that allows my spirit to be completely crushed without also suffering terrible confusion and fear?

THE WISDOM OF LAOTSE

Chinese wisdom about life and death can be found more in the works of Laotse—born in 571 B.C. and a contemporary of Confucius—than in the works of Confucius himself. Laotse was a poet, while Confucius was a social philosopher. Like most poetry, Laotse's admitted a variety of interpretations. It wasn't until about 300 B.C. that Chuang-Tzu wrote his famous commentaries on the wisdom of Laotse. The passage below is taken from Chuang-Tzu's commentaries.

Laotse sees life and death with agnostic eyes. We don't really know whether "life" as we talk about it is just a dream we're having. We don't really know what happens after we die—whether we return and, if we do, what path we take. We don't even know whether "we" are anything. Look at the phenomenon of a smile. Smiling occurs when pleasure happens; no thought of "ours" is necessary. So is it really "we" who are smiling or is this "we" just an illusion we need to talk about as the carrier of a smile smiling itself?

This profound resignation in the face of death and the totally ironic view of the self can seem unreasonable. Yet there is no proof that this view is wrong. What is more, this kind of resignation is supported only by the fact that people who live it out are always admired by others. That is, men and women who take this view to heart seem to suffer far less anxiety than those who, as we would say today, are "into control."

Listen to Laotse, through the words of Chuang-Tzu, and hear the peace of resignation:

> [Confucius said,] "Human life in this world is but as the form of a white pony flashing across a rock crevice. In a moment it is gone. Suddenly, waking up, all life is born. Suddenly, slipping off, all silently creep away.
>
> "With one change, one is born. With another, one dies. Living creatures moan and humankind weeps. Remove its bondage, slipping off its skin carcass and curling up, where shall the soul of a person go and the body go with it? Is it perhaps on the great journey home?
>
> Yen Huei said to Confucius, "When Mengsun Ts'ai's mother died, he wept but without sniveling. His heart was not grieved. He wore mourning but without sorrow. Yet, while wanting on these three points he is considered the best mourner in the state of Lu. Can there be really people with a hollow reputation? I am astonished."
>
> "Mr. Mengsun—," said Confucius, "Mr. Mengsun has really mastered the Tao. He has gone beyond the wise ones. There are still some things he cannot quite give up but he has already given up certain things. Mr. Mengsun knows not whence we come in life nor whither we go in death. He knows not which to put first and which to put last. He is ready to be transformed into other things, without caring into what he may be transformed. That is all. How could that which is changing say that it could not change? And how could that which regards itself as permanent realize that it is changing already? Even you and I are perhaps dreamers who have not yet awakened. Moreover, he knows his form is subject to change. But his mind remains the same. He believes not in real death but regards it as moving into a new house. He weeps only when he sees others weep—as it comes to him naturally.
>
> "Besides, we all talk of 'me.' How do you know what is this 'me' that we speak of? You dream you are a bird and soar to heaven, or dream you are a fish and dive into the ocean depths. And you cannot tell whether the man now speaking is awake or in a dream. A woman feels a

pleasurable sensation before she smiles. And smiles before she thinks how she ought to smile. Resign yourself to the sequences of things, forgetting the changes of life and you shall enter into the pure, the divine, the one."

Here the only constant in life is change. Some are births and some are deaths. The sense of being oneself is ultimately an illusion that accompanies the brief flash between appearing and disappearing. People who ask where they go after death beg the question, since there really is no "they" to go anywhere.

This is a healthy contemplation because it shakes our certainty that our egos or selves are real. Like many other explanations of how the world works, the evidence does not indisputably support the idea that this "I" (of which I so easily speak) is objectively real. It is just as possible that "I" am being dreamed by some other entity, or that the very smiles "I" smile are fluctuations in the sequence of things that carry an illusory and quite temporary sense of self.

Still, it is difficult for Westerners to abandon the sense of self. It is apparently difficult even for the most experienced practitioners in Eastern religions. Is enlightenment a matter of breaking through to the minority view? If so, who am "I" that is enlightened to see there is no "I"? That is, should we hope someday to be able to say, paradoxically, "I realized that 'I' don't exist"? On the other hand, if enlightenment is a matter of clinging to the belief that I am a real, existing entity, then what would protect me from the human fate of continually worrying and fretting about myself?

This contemplation contains another proposition that deserves attention. It is the idea that there is an objective process going on that carries us along—this is the fundamental idea in Hegel's philosophy of history. Just as our pets live in a world far bigger than they realize, so we may be living in a far bigger world. Is this true? If we believe it, can we say anything about this larger world, or are we as blind to it as a goldfish is oblivious of a mortgage? If nothing else, at least his contemplation reminds us that the obvious may not be everything. It may even lighten our grip on the selves we so spontaneously protect.

THE BOOK OF JOB

While Chuang-Tzu was teaching these doctrines in a philosophic voice, Hebrews were grappling with the idea of realities larger than our lives in a more narrative mode, as we can see in the Book of Job.

The Book of Job reads like the script of a play, which it may well have been. It was written around the beginning of the 5th century B.C., about the same time that Chuang-Tzu lived and long before any Hebrews gave serious thought to the idea of an afterlife. Most of the Hebrew bible makes no mention of an afterlife, and the most-cited references in the Psalms (6, 22, 28, 88) show little more than a common assumption that after death a person goes to "Sheol," a land of shadows. Hebrews made no connection between moral living and spiritual fate in a next life—an alleged oversight that Christians find baffling and Moslems find heretical. Instead, moral living was connected directly to the historical relationship between the Jewish people and Yahweh, their God. This relationship was established and defined by the strongest known legal document of the time—the covenant.

The covenant was essentially a promise, initiated by Yahweh, to guard and foster the Hebrew tribes. Its terms were social, not individual. Being moral meant creating an entire community in which Yahweh's earliest command to be fruitful and multiply would be carried out. The essential divine vocation for any person was simply to live as a good Jew. The sanction for the individual to be good had nothing to do with heavenly reward. Instead, everything had to do with racial survival and even supremacy.

During the five centuries before Christ, however, the Promised Land of the Hebrews happened to contain major commercial crossroads for Greeks, Romans, Mesopotamians, and Egyptians. It is the nature of commerce to exchange not only goods but also ideas, and however strongly the Hebrews clung to their traditional beliefs they could not boycott the ideas of an afterlife marketed by other cultures. It is evident that even by the time of Christ, the Sadducee party rejected the idea of an afterlife while the Pharisees accepted it—a division exploited by Paul as recorded in Acts of the Apostles.

In this passage from *Job*, there are hints that the author has heard that some people believe in an afterlife. Still, he doubts that they are right. Even when he speculates about what an afterlife might be for, he does not talk about enjoying some justifying reward in heaven for his this-worldly troubles. Nor does he talk about spending a next life with God. Rather, he heads in the direction of getting even with his enemies on earth. It is revenge that makes him imagine what an afterlife might give him.

These are not unfamiliar sentiments to anyone who believes in God's care, yet is a victim of continual misfortune. And, after all, has anyone yet really justified this arrangement in which our goodness seems completely irrelevant to our happiness? In the end, Job settles for a simple belief, standing on faith, that God's judgment will somehow come, although he cannot explain his belief any further than that.

And that judgment is less a matter of divine approval as justification in the eyes of his earthly adversaries.

Still, in this respect, Job reveals how bare the essentials of faith really are. The "Yes, I trust God," small and inexplicable though it be, stands firm against the accusations of skeptics that there is no evidence for this belief, and even against the accusations of his skeptical heart that the evidence of misfortune mounts higher by the day. Here, then, is Job:

> Since I have lost all taste for life, I will give free rein to my complaints; I shall let my embittered soul speak out.
>
> I shall say to God, "Do not condemn me, but tell me the reason for your assault! Is it right for you to injure me, cheapening the work of your own hands and abetting the schemes of the wicked? Have you got human eyes, do you see as we see? Is your life mortal like ours, do your years pass as our days pass?"
>
> "You, who inquire into my faults and investigate my sins, you know very well that I am innocent and that no one can rescue me from your hand. Your own hands shaped me, modelled me; and would you now have second thoughts, and destroy me? . . .
>
> "Why did you bring me out of the womb? I should have perished then, unseen by any eye—a being that had never been, to be carried from womb to grave. The days of my life are few enough; turn your eyes away, leave me a little joy, before I go to the place of no return, the land of murk and deep shadow, where dimness and disorder hold sway, and light itself is like the dead of night.
>
> "We, once in our resting place, will never rise again. The heavens will wear away before we wake, before we rise from our sleep. If only you would hide me in Sheol, and shelter me there until your anger is past, fixing a certain day for calling me to mind—for once someone is dead, is there any return to life?—day after day of my service I would wait for my relief to come. Then you would call, and I should answer, you would want to see the work of your hands once more. Now you count every step I take, but then you would cease to spy on my sins; You would seal up my crime in a bag and whiten my fault over.
>
> "But no! Soon or late the mountain falls, the rock moves from its place, water wears away the stones, the cloudburst erodes the soil; just so do you destroy our hope. You crush us

once for all, and we are gone; you mar us, and then you bid us go. Let our children achieve honour, and we do not know of it; humiliation, we give it not a thought. We feel no pain for anything but our own body, make no lament save for our own life. . . .

Ah, would that these words of mine were written down, inscribed on some monument with iron chisel and engraving tool, cut into the rock forever:

> 'I know that my avenger lives, and he, the last, will take his stand on earth! After my awaking, he will set me close to him, and from my flesh I shall look on God. He whom I shall see will take my part: these eyes will gaze on him and find him not aloof. My heart within me sinks . . .'

You then that mutter, "How shall we track him down, what pretext shall we find against him?" may well fear the sword on your own account. There is an anger stirred to flame by evil deeds; you will learn that there is indeed a judgment."

How can we account for Job's faith here? He really does not believe God will raise him up after death, although he expresses his complaint in a classic Jewish hyperbolic request that carries a hint of "if only" between the lines of apparent despair—think of Tevya singing "If I were a rich man" in *Fiddler on the Roof*. This is not even faith that all shall turn out well, even though Job's fate does turn out well. It is rather a faith that God will continue to be in conversation and, while marring individuals and then bidding them go, that God will be faithful to the larger Jewish community.

It is because Job belongs to the tribe that Job has a deep relationship with God. Job himself makes it clear that he trusts in God not because of any past or future good fortune. Job acts like a man under a King who does what he pleases but who at least talks to his subjects.

What we are left to contemplate, then, is how our own faith may not be as individualized as we imagine. Indeed most of us inherited our faith. We make it our own, certainly, but we shouldn't overlook the possibility that our faith is essentially a community's possession, not an individual's. There's a story in Mark's Gospel about a crippled man being let down through the roof to the feet of Jesus for a cure. Jesus cures the man after "seeing their faith"—not the man's faith, but the faith of his friends.

Is your faith weak or strong? To a great extent, the answer depends on taking "your" as plural. If you take it as plural, then perhaps you can relax about your personal death. Your life's concern, like Job's, might well be more directed toward building up the faith of those you call your own. It is their faith that counts, along with yours, because the death of a community of faith is the far larger tragedy.

THE HINDU UPANISHADS

In Hinduism we find an even more clear expression of the idea that human life is encompassed by something larger. It is a central belief of Hinduism is that an objective spirit called Brahman governs all existence. That is, every individual thing partakes in a larger, universal and highly spiritual process. This participation occurs in two modes—in consciousness and in space. "We should consider that in the inner world Brahman is consciousness; and we should consider that in the outer world Brahman is space. These are the two meditations."

In the domain of consciousness, what counts is living in the truth, doing good deeds, and bearing compassion toward all creatures as embodiments of that same, common Brahman. What doesn't count, therefore, is any anxiety or worry about the future, including one's death. Death is regarded simply as an element in world process. One lives best by going with the flow of life's natural cycles. In theory, nothing should ever be disappointing or deserving of fear.

This is the foundation for the Hindu belief in the continuous cycles of reincarnation. Those individuals whose lives are beset with worry, ambition, hatred, and excessive desire bring that nest of confusion to their deaths and, because they do, they cannot find rest in Brahman because Brahman does not recognize such a soul. So they return to earth in another embodiment because their concerns have yet to be released from earth, having failed to find this liberation of soul during that lifetime.

Frankly, I don't believe there's much fruit in thinking about the process of reincarnation. Granted, we enjoy the discussions about what we'd like to come back as. But by itself, the doctrine of reincarnation cannot convey the full significance of the Hindu doctrine about Brahman. It is more like a logical corollary—like the Catholic doctrine about purgatory—designed to respond to the question about what happens to immoral or ambitious people after death.

The richer fruit lies in asking ourselves whether or not there really is an objective "spirit" or "process" going on in the universe. This larger-than-life reality would be personal in itself and would show itself everywhere—in every event in human psyches and in every event in time and space. We certainly have evidence that absolutely invisible, inaudible, intangible events occur—our every thought, feeling, judgment, and commitment. So reality does not seem to be restricted to what is manifest through our five senses. But even after we recognize the reality of these spiritual occurrences within us, the question remains whether or not they are evidence that we participate in a yet larger reality. Even after we acknowledge that it is our thinking, feeling, judging, and committing that make up the substance of human togetherness and the making of our history, we can ask whether they are, at the same time, experiences of a personal entity that lives in the universe of all things real.

See, in this text from the *Upanishads*, whether or not this may be true.

> OM: In the centre of the castle of Brahman, our own body, there is a small shrine in the form of a lotus-flower, and within can be found a small space. We should find who dwells there, and we should want to know him.
>
> And if anyone asks, "Who is he who dwells in a small shrine in the form of a lotus-flower in the centre of the castle of Brahman? Whom should we want to find and to know?" we can answer:
>
> "The little space within the heart is as great as this vast universe. The heavens and the earth are there, and the sun, and the moon, and the stars; fire and lightning and winds are there; and all that now is and all that is not: for the whole universe is in Him and He dwells within our heart."
>
> And if they should say, "If all things are in the castle of Brahman, all beings and all desires, what remains when old age overcomes the castle or when the life of the body is gone?" we can answer:
>
> "The Spirit who is in the body does not grow old and does not die, and no one can ever kill the Spirit who is everlasting. This is the real castle of Brahman wherein dwells all the love of the universe. It is Atman, pure Spirit, beyond sorrow, old age, and death; beyond evil and hunger and thirst. It is Atman whose love is Truth, whose thoughts are Truth."
>
> Even as here on earth the attendants of a king obey their king, and are with him wherever he is and go with him wherever he goes, so all love which is Truth and all thoughts of Truth obey the Atman, the Spirit. And even as here on earth all work done in time ends in time, so in the worlds to come even the good works of the past pass away. Therefore

those who leave this world and have not found their soul,
and that love which is Truth, find not their freedom in other
worlds. But those who leave this world and have found their
soul and that love which is Truth, for them there is the
liberty of the spirit, in this world and in the worlds to come.

So, did you recognize this spirit? Underneath the metaphors of lotus flower and castle, is there a reality within each of us that is larger than any one of us? And isn't this spiritual reality a spirit of Truth and Love? Isn't this really a Someone and not just a Something?

And in the outer world, the world we think of as spatial, is there a reality that is invisible and not confined to spatial categories? Something that encompasses all the planets and stars in the universe? And isn't this reality intelligent? Isn't this really a Someone and not a Something?

If both consciousness and space put us in touch with what is larger than us, then what about our death? Hindu teaching says that those who knowingly embrace this larger reality during life become that reality in death. In this view, I become part of a universal consciousness and part of universal space. Death becomes a lifting up, an absorption, an expansion, an exalted destiny. Those who do not embrace it have failed to embrace both the full capacities of their consciousness and the full significance and meaning of the created universe. Their death is the death of an incomplete spirit that lived in a partial world. There get no second chance in any post-death purgatory to expand to their fullest potential. What they made of themselves is finished and complete, with no chance to liberate this particular body. Logically, it seems best to suppose a kind of return in another body, but with the same unfinished spirit seeking the fuller world, and under completely unforeseen and different circumstances.

Whether or not we accept this entire view, we cannot help but mull over the awesome possibility that what I make of myself in this particular body may be complete at death. Neither a Purgatory, a Transmigration, nor God's forgiveness will not change the reality of what I made of myself. Death then lays a demand on faith. It requires that my faith not count on anything beyond Death. It must count on how I live my life.

THE HINDU BHAGAVAD GITA

The following texts are taken from the *Bhagavad Gita* or "Song of the Lord." They were composed between the 5th and 2nd centuries B.C. They speak of the way God loves the individual and of how the individual can best receive that love. What is important to contemplate here is the ultimately personal nature of whatever larger entity encompasses human life.

In our own time, many people consider themselves spiritual without being religious. They believe we experience spiritual events but they do not go so far as affirming a personal source of those events. No doubt they have considered the arguments in favor of God. They know the logic that says the laws of the universe must have an intelligent source. But argument based on logic is not convincing because conviction requires not simply an intellectual judgment like "It makes sense." It also requires a personal commitment like "I will follow."

In the *Gita*, however, Brahman is presented neither as a clever inventor nor an impersonal world process but as a warm and tender lover, beckoning the individual to an intimate union and promising a release from the trials of everyday life. This loving union begins in this life and carries the devoted Hindu across death's threshold into complete union with Brahman. Read the following passage, then, not as an explanation but as an invitation. It should appeal not to your mind's need for truth but rather to your heart's need for company.

> Thus the wisdom, more secret than all secrets, has been declared to thee by Me. Having considered it fully, do as thou choosest. Hear again My supreme word, the most secret of all: Thou are greatly beloved my Me, hence I will speak for thy good.
>
> Center thy mind on Me, be devoted to Me, sacrifice to Me, revere Me, and thou shalt come to Me. I promise thee truly, for thou are dear to Me. Abandoning all other duties, come to Me alone for refuge. I shall free thee from all sins: be not grieved.
>
> He attains peace into whom all desires flow as waters into the sea which, though ever being filled, is ever motionless; and not he who lusts after desires. She who abandons all desires and acts without longing, without self-interest or egotism, she attains peace. This is the eternal state, O Partha (Arjuna); having attained it, one is no longer confused. Fixed in it even at the time of death, one attains to the bliss of Brahman.
>
> The foolish think of Me, the unmanifest, as having only come into manifestation; not knowing My higher nature which is immutable and supreme. I am not revealed to all, being covered by My power of illusion. This world is deluded and does not recognize Me, the unborn and imperishable.

I know beings that are past, that are present and that are yet to be, O Arjuna, but no one knows Me. All beings are born to confusion, O Bharata, and are deluded by the dualities that originate from desire and hatred, O conqueror of the foe.

But those of virtuous deeds whose sins are ended and who are freed from the delusion of opposites worship Me with steadfast resolve. Those who strive for liberation from old age and death and have taken refuge in Me know Brahman entirely and the supreme Self and all action. Those who know Me together with material and divine domains and the highest sacrifice; they, of balanced mind, know Me even at the time of death.

She who controls the gates of the body, confines the mind in the heart, places the breath in the head, establishes herself in concentration by yoga, pronounces the single syllable, "Om," which is Brahman, meditates on Me as she goes forth and abandons the body, she reaches her highest goal.

He who always thinks of Me and not of something else, for him, O Partha, who is a yogin ever disciplined, I am easy to obtain.

Having come to Me, these great-souled ones do not attain rebirth, the place of sorrow and impermanence, for they have reached the highest perfection. From the world of Brahma downwards, all worlds are reborn, O Arjuna; but having come to Me, O son of Kunti, there is no rebirth.

So? Do you feel the attraction? Do you experience a deep yearning for "liberation"? Do you find that this invitation to simplicity awakens something very good in you? Weren't you attracted by the possibility of going to death without fear? And not merely without fear but almost with an enthusiasm to meet One who invites you? Are you invited, then? Is there Someone who wants you?

One proposition to contemplate here is whether or not our reality is encompassed not just by universal laws but by a divine Someone. And even if answers to that question are not forthcoming, at least we must admit that the *question* of God belongs to human nature, no matter what answer you or I embrace.

A BUDDHIST LIBERATED FROM REGRET

This is a story of a man who commits suicide. It's a disturbing story because there is no hint that his suicide might be unreasonable, given the circumstances. Nor is there any glimmer of hope that there's another life after this one. But it's a good story because it turns our attention away from the general questions about the ethics of suicide and what happens at death and puts the focus instead on how the prospect of death intensifies that dark emotion simmering in all of us: regret.

There are three kinds of regrets. The obvious kind is the regret we feel over some damage we did to another person, some lie, some theft. A less obvious kind is when fear held back our hand from someone in need or held back our voice when another's lie was spreading. The third kind has nothing to do with wrongful action or wrongful inaction. It is the regret we feel that we never pursued our dream.

By "dream" I mean not some vision of how we hope the world to be. I mean a desire that we carry in our hearts and that won't go away. For example, a desire to visit a long-lost friend, a desire to take up art, a desire to meet our favorite author, a desire to celebrate our marriage with a huge party, a desire to write poetry, a desire to be alone for a few months. There seems to be nothing morally wrong about *not* doing these things, and yet, to the degree that these desires come out of our best selves, we feel the sting of conscience nonetheless.

Moreover, while forgiveness can heal the first two kinds of regret, it cannot heal the regret that we did not follow our dream with single-mindedness. Logically, I am the only one who can forgive me because I am the only injured party. But when I try to forgive myself, I in effect violate my dream. I simply cannot tell myself that it's OK that I never took up the clarinet if I dreamt about it since grade school and still thrill at its sound.

Some years ago, I learned I had cancer. For two weeks, while waiting for a complete prognosis, all my type-three regrets rose up—all the things that I could never do if my cancer was terminal. Interestingly, I regretted less the stupid and self-centered things I have done. Perhaps because they were beyond my power to change. Perhaps because I long ago was reconciled to the idea that only others can forgive me. But my regret at having been too lazy or fearful to welcome more deeply what life offers brought on a profound shame. Is there any healing of this kind of regret?

Yes, it occurs in the following story. Valkali was a disciple of the Buddha who, during his lifetime, often dreamed of making the journey to see the Buddha in person. When he fell mortally ill, he had great regrets that he had never made the journey. When the Buddha then made the journey to visit him, he felt doubly bad. But the Buddha explained something to him which gave Valkali the moral strength to let go of his regret.

Valkali, a disciple of the Buddha, fell sick and was in great pain. The Buddha was informed, and he came to Valkali's side. The man's conscience is clear, but he has an unfulfilled desire—before he died, he wanted to see the Buddha.

The master approached and said to him: "Do not move, Valkali, there are seats quite near, and I shall sit there." Having sat down, he went on, "Friend, is it tolerable? Is it viable? Are the painful feelings you are experiencing on the decrease and not on the increase?"

"No, Master," replied Valkali, "it is neither tolerable nor viable. The painful feelings are on the increase and not on the decrease."

"Then you have some regret and some remorse?"

"Yes, Master," confessed Valkali, "I have much regret and much remorse."

"Does you conscience reproach you for something from the moral point of view?"

"No, my conscience does not reproach me for anything from the moral point of view."

"And yet," stated the Buddha, "you have regret and remorse."

"This is because for a long time I have wanted to go and look at the Master, but I do not find the strength in my body to do it."

"For shame, Valkali!" cried the Buddha, "What good would it do you to see my body of filth? Valkali, whoever sees my Doctrine, sees me; whoever sees me sees my Doctrine."

Having spoken thus, the Buddha went to the Vulture Peak, while Valkali had himself carried to the Black Rock on the Seers' Mount. During the night two deities warned the Buddha that Valkali was thinking of liberating himself and that, once liberated, he would be delivered.

The Buddha dispatched some monks to Valkali to tell him: "Blameless will be your death, blameless the end of your days."

"Return to your Master," said Valkali, "and in my name prostrate yourselves at his feet. Be sure and tell him that I no longer feel any doubt regarding the transitory, painful and unstable nature of all the phenomena of existence."

The monks had hardly left when Valkali 'took the knife' and killed himself. The Buddha, being doubtful about this, immediately went to the Black Rock in the company of several disciples. Valkali lay dying on his couch, his shoulders turned to the right, for it is thus that the Noble Ones die. A cloud of black dust moved around him.

"Do you see, O Monks," the Buddha asked, "that cloud of dust which is drifting in all directions around the corpse? It is Mara, the Malign One who is seeking the whereabouts of Valkali's consciousness. But Valkali's consciousness is nowhere: Valkali is in complete Nirvana."

Hence the Noble Ones who have triumphed over delusion and eliminated passion can, once their task is done, speed the hour of deliverance by voluntarily taking their own lives. Whatever the means used, act of will, recourse to the supernormal, or quite simply the rope or knife, their suicide is "blameless."

What liberated Valkali was not any ascetic self-denial that suppressed his dream of seeing the Buddha. Nor was it the sight of Buddha, since his dream was to make the journey himself, not have the Buddha come to him. The Buddha simply explained to him that he already had possession of the kernal of his dream. That is, by embracing the Buddha's teachings, he already possessed everything of value which the Buddha could give had Valkali made the journey. It was an enlightenment, a revelation, an insight, a realization. It was an act of the mind, not of the will and not of any direct experience.

The lesson here may be phrased as follows: Follow your dream, but follow it inward first. That is, find what lies at the kernal of your desire; go there first and discover what it is that you really seek. Let your heart reveal itself, but be aware that this requires asking questions. Enlightenment, after all, is unlike the illumination we receive when we light a candle. It is rather the result of a search, and a search always starts with a question. Only then can any external journey be successful. In most cases, you will find that you already possess what you seek.

LESSON FOR A BUDDHIST NOVICE

Buddhism is not a religion, at least not in the sense of an institution based on belief in God. It is rather a body of doctrine and discipline on how to live. An essential doctrine is the simple fact that we shall die. Buddhist discipline involves frequent meditation on this fact. So novices ("Bhikkhs") in a Buddhist monastery spend many hours nourishing the practical awareness that they will die. They are taught simple contemplative exercises, such as spending an hour repeating two sentences, "Death will take place. The life faculty will be interrupted." Or simply repeating "Death. Death."

They are also taught meditative exercises in which they think about the significance of death. For example, one lesson is that because everyone dies, so everyone must accept the fact that life is ultimately disenchanting. Nothing is permanent. True, these thoughts stir up expectation of pain. They remind us that our selfhood—about which we have cared every conscious minute—comes to an end. Even so, there is no reason to fear—not because these threats are illusory but, on the contrary, because they are implacable. There is no reason to add the pain of fear to the pain that will come in any case.

The realization that I will die is a wet bar of soap. We can hold it lightly, but it easily slips out of consciousness. I can make an unequivocal statement such as "Yes, I will die," but that doesn't mean that I have realized the truth of it. When I was in seventh grade, a priest had been invited in to talk about God's final judgment. "Actuarial tables predict one of us would be dead in 20 years," he said. "In 30 years, three of us would be dead. In 40 years, 10 of us. In 60 years," he said, "half the class would be dead." Then he asked, "Raise your hand if you picture yourself as one of the survivors." Naturally, 100 percent of us raised our hands. It is practically impossible to realize "I" will die.

The reason it is so difficult to realize "I" will die is that it is impossible to imagine ourselves *not* experiencing anything, not watching, not thinking, not feeling, not tasting, not hearing. Even if we picture ourselves in a coma, we are picturing ourselves. We are watching this scene. But the body rots, and if the body rots, then human experiencing ends. In a very ordinary sense, our spirits collapse. We cannot look at ourselves dying because looking dies as we do.

Children typically are easier with death than adults are. Matty Ventresca did not seem to be afraid of death, despite his knowledge that dying would be painful. It is more likely that because Matty's adoptive parents knew from the beginning that his life would be short, they taught Matty that death is going to be part of his life before long. Few children Matty's age have to make that act of acceptance. But his parents' acceptance taught Matty in a short time what it would take a long time for a Buddhist novice director to teach a Buddhist novice.

Here, then, is an excerpt from Buddhist instructions to would-be monks. As you read, you may find that the teachings here were well known to Matty.

> Bhikkhs devoted to the mindfulness of death are constantly diligent. They acquire perception of disenchantment with all kinds of "becoming" (existence). They conquer

attachment to life. They condemn evil. They avoid much storing. They have no state of avarice about requisites. Perception of impermanence grows in them, following upon which appear the perceptions of pain and not-self. But while beings who have not developed mindfulness of death fall victims to fear, horror and confusion at the time of death—as though suddenly seized by wild beasts, spirits, snakes, robbers or murderers—those mindful of death die undeluded and fearless without falling into any such state. And if they do not attain the deathless here and now, they are at least headed for a happy destiny on the breakup of the body.

Now, when you are truly wise, your constant task will surely be this recollection about death, blessed with such mighty potency.

Novices were also taught various ways of meditating on death. In each way, the meditator was to make a comparison, an analogy, in order to deepen awareness of what death is about.

1. As having the ruthlessness of a murderer.
2. As being the ruin of any success.
3. By comparison with how even the famous, the worthy, the strong, the wise, and even the fully enlightened Buddhas die.
4. On how the dead body will be shared by "eighty families of worms."
5. On the frailty of life in general.
6. On the unpredictability of when and how death occurs.
7. On the shortness and "death" of each present moment.

Here is the text on #2, that death is the ruin of any success:

All health ends in sickness. All youth ends in aging. All life ends in death.

All worldly existence is procured by birth, haunted by ageing, surprised by sickness and struck down by death. As it is said,

As though huge mountains made of rock, so vast they reached up to the sky, were to advance from every side, grinding beneath them all that lives,
So age and death roll over all—warriors, priests, merchants and craftsmen, the outcasts and the scavengers—crushing all beings, sparing none.

And here no troops of elephants, no charioteers, no infantry, no strategy in form of spells or riches serve to beat them off.

This is how death should be recollected as the "ruin of success" by defining it as death's final ruining of life's success.

These meditations are not really about death. They are about life. Look again at the seven topics listed above. They present a kind of diamond with seven facets that we spontaneously identify with the "good life": Vitality, Success, Fame, Health, Strength, Foresight, and Permanence. To the Buddhist, this diamond is fake, and it takes the light of Death to realize it. "Those mindful of death die undeluded and fearless."

THE CHRISTIAN ACTS OF THE APOSTLES

This text is taken from the opening of Luke's work, *Acts of the Apostles*. Although he finished it about thirty years after the death of Jesus, he relies on accounts of the first Christian homily, preached by Peter, as well as on a speculative, but intriguing, narrative about Jesus' own thoughts about dying.

The question of an afterlife was very popular in Jerusalem at this time. Yet, despite the popularity of the belief that everyone goes on to an afterlife, Peter assumes that Jesus alone was favored by God with a next life. By pointing out that even King David was not raised, he shows his belief that the resurrection does not belong to the natural order of things but rather to the free choice of a personal God. In Luke's eyes, the hope of Jesus himself was not based on a belief in a general resurrection but rather in his personal relationship with God.

Today, Christian faith in the resurrection commonly is reduced to a scripted play in which we are born, die, and then head off to our reward or punishment. However, there is little evidence that this was the original belief of Christians. Being Jewish, they inherited a belief in a God who changes his mind, a God unnervingly free and at times capricious.

Luke presents Jesus' own thoughts about dying as thoughts of any human who, ultimately, has nothing but faith to rely on. Jesus of Nazareth is a person who kept God in mind always and could not believe that this God would sever this loving relationship. Jesus so personalized the divine as to prefer the name "Father," or "Daddy" ("Abba"). What counted was less his personal survival through death and more the survival of his intimate and loving relationship to this

Father. The alternative was that his flesh would rot and his soul would slip away to Sheol, a kind of limbo that had nothing to do with either punishment or reward. Jesus simply could not believe that God, whom he kept before his eyes always, would let him sink into mortal oblivion.

Luke must have undergone a profound enlightenment about death. Early Christians believed not only that God raised this man up and gave him the divine name and status, but also that Jesus, now with God, poured out the divine Spirit on all his followers. Although this flooding the disciples' hearts with the divine Spirit had the immediate effect of energizing them to preach the gospel to people beyond the borders of Judaism, it also was a pledge from Jesus that the disciples too would be raised up by the Father in the same way he was. The meaning of life was no longer confined to this earth, sloping off to an ethereal existence after death. They began to call life *this* life, in contrast to a "life to come." In the life to come, as living already in God's Spirit, they would be gathered into God's bosom as friends of Jesus.

I suggest that you read the text below and put yourself in the position of Jesus: On the one hand, he is a man who did not consider an afterlife as part of the natural order. He is a Jew who so revered the transcendence of God that he would not presume to expect that God owed humanity any promise of eternal bliss. On the other hand, he is so tenderly consumed with love for God that he is incapable of believing he will be an abandoned child. (We can only wonder how profound must have been his relationship to Joseph, whom he also called "Daddy.") He feels an exquisite tension of faith in which his religious heritage keeps an awesome distance from God yet his personal experience draws him intimately close. As I say, put yourself into the position of Jesus, recalling that tension in yourself between feeling distant from and yet proximate to the divine. See if anything in you resonates with the psalm Jesus prays, "I saw the Lord before me always . . ."

Here, then, is Peter's homily as recorded by Luke:

> "Fellow Israelites, listen! As you know, Jesus the Nazarene was a man commended to you by God through the miracles, the wonders and the signs that God worked through him when he was among you. You took this man, delivered up by the deliberate purpose and foreknowledge of God, handed him over to people outside the Law, and by crucifixion put him to death. He is the one God raised to life, freeing him from the throes of death; for it was impossible for him to be held in its power since, as David says of him:

I saw the Lord before me always, for with him at my right hand nothing can disturb me.

So my heart was glad and my lips sung for joy; my flesh too will abide in the hope that you will not abandon my soul to Sheol nor let your Holy One to experience corruption.

As you have made known the way of life to me, so will you fill me with joy through your presence.

Friends, I tell you plainly, the patriarch David is dead and buried. His tomb is with us today. But since he was a prophet, he knew that God had sworn him an oath to make the fruit of his loins succeed him on the throne. What he foresaw and spoke about was the resurrection of the Christ: he is the one what was "not abandoned to Sheol," and whose flesh did not "experience corruption". God raised this Jesus to life. We are witnesses to that. Moreover, raised to God's right hand and having received from the Father the promised Holy Spirit, what you see and hear [the disciples speaking in tongues] is the outpouring of that Spirit.

Those in the audience who took this message seriously had to embrace a completely different view of death. They had to feel invited by God to follow Jesus through their deaths into the same place where Jesus went. Death became a total act of trust in an invitation Jesus gave them. Death meant entering into a trustful waiting for God's free initiative. This faith in God and in the promise of Jesus is total because it was not at all supported by the notion that a next life awaits us all. So the faith with which they met death was faith in Someone's pledge—a highly personal, intimate, and trusting response to an invitation.

THE MUSLIM KORAN

The human search for God is driven by two forces which we may call tradition and inspiration. Although the many ways they play off each other show in the variety of religions woven into the fabric of our history, the underlying dynamic is the same. Traditions are born in inspiration, but, once established, tradition tends to stifle inspiration. Those religions that favor inspiration tend to pop up suddenly, in many cases as a reaction to a stifling tradition. They gather a small, zealous following, but then they vanish. Wary of traditionalism, they fail to create the institutions needed to pass on their own tradition to the next generation. On the other hand, religions that favor tradition tend to endure because their originating inspiration was narrated, codified, and supported by schools, scholars, and lawyers. Their words, perspectives, and values are developed in a give-and-take with an entire social order, so that the religion becomes a cultural mainstay. Unfortunately, they also tend to clad the founding experiences in rigid concepts and rules. As a result, latter-day followers adhere to creed, code, and cult without understanding the living inspirations from which the religion sprung. Without that familiarity with the originating inspiration, they lack the means—and so the incentives—for adapting old ways to new needs.

Of the two paths—tradition and inspiration—Islam certainly favors tradition as the appropriate vehicle for reaching the divine. Indeed, its very foundation was a body of teaching, not any inspirational event. Mohammed was not a martyr or sacrificial lamb; he did not claim that God's Spirit possessed him. He considered himself a teacher and prophet—a specialist in words. Today, its authoritarian style is familiar to everyone, particularly in various forms of Islamic militancy.

Most Christians will find no objection to the text below, since it supports a belief in an afterlife. Still, there is a presumption here that can go unnoticed. For Islam, the afterlife is part of God's original and eternal plan. It belongs to the natural order of things. Original Christianity, as we saw, taught that the resurrection from the dead was *not* part of an eternal, immutable order of things. Rather, it was a special act of God beginning something unprecedented in history—the raising of Jesus to shared divinity and the pledge to Jesus' faithful followers of the same.

The text that follows, taken from the Koran, presents a debate between divine messengers and human skeptics. Notice the presumption that God created a universe on two planes—a "this world" and a "next world." Your actions in this world determined your status in the next. Notice especially your personal reaction to this authoritarian style of governance and ask, "Is this the God I believe in?" Or, if you are skeptical about a "next life," ask yourself, "Does my antipathy toward this teaching mean that there cannot be a 'next life' in any sense?"

The passage begins with the divine messengers speaking:

> Unbelievers say, "What! When we are dead and have become dust, shall we be raised up again? That's impossible!"
> We, the divine messengers, know exactly how much the earth diminishes us but how much it increases us as well. For with us is the Book of Deeds, and it preserves everything.

> Unbelievers rejected the truth when it came to them. This is why they have everything mixed up. They should look at the sky above, how we have spread it out and adorned it. They will find no flaws. They should look at the earth below, how we have laid it down and put great mountains on it. They will find here every kind of beautiful plant that should enlighten them and remind them that all nature turns to God—the blessings of water from the sky, the abundance of gardens and harvests, the way tall palm trees reach out, one branch high, the next branch higher. All this lifts up an otherwise dead land and provides for humanity. That is how it will be in the Resurrection.
>
> Not that we have become unsatisfied with the creation of earth. No, what unbelievers are confused about is the new creation.
>
> Know this: We created humanity. We know every whispered thought in every mind. We are closer to you than your jugular vein. We have two Recording Angels writing everything down, one on your right, the other on your left. There's not a word you say that a guardian angel doesn't record.
>
> When the shadow of death overtakes you, you will hear, "This is what you were running from." And you will also hear, "This is the Day of Promise." On that day, every soul will come out, accompanied by one angel ready to witness why you should be in Hell and another angel ready to witness why you should be in Heaven.
>
> Then we will say, "You paid no attention to this. But now we have lifted the veil, and your eyes are exceedingly sharp."

It would be difficult to tell whether Matty and his family held a belief about an afterlife that was closer to Islamic or to Christian teachings. In one sense, it makes no difference in their moral life. They inherited the common Christian belief that if they are not good in this life, the next will be hell. Yet in another sense, their view of God does make a difference to their religious life. Religion is more than morality, after all. It expects people to live moral lives but for reasons based on loving relations between creator and creatures, rather than on reasons based solely on how humans ought to get along together. In both Islam and Christianity, God is portrayed using the model of a paternally structured family. God is the father, the one who makes the decisions and provides for the children. Yet the styles of divine fatherhood differ. In Islam, the Father is constant, fair, and directive to the point of being overbearing. In Christianity, as least as revealed in accounts of Jesus' spirituality, the Father is shifting, one-sided, and so merciful that his justice seems secondary.

As for Matty, whichever Father he may have imagined in heaven, at his age he probably believed that his afterlife was part of the natural order of things rather than a free and always unique gift of God—much as any child believes that parents will always provide, without noticing the free and difficult choices those parents make. Had he lived into adulthood, though, he surely would have learned about the sacrifices his parents made on his behalf, sacrifices that were freely given, not just automatic in the process of growing up. And that realization about his parents' love may well have taught him that his Father in heaven will welcome him there out of a love freely given, and not out of a submission to some higher law of fate.

Then Matty would have to forgive God. That forgiveness would not be necessary were his handicap merely blind fate, part of the randomness of nature. But if it was fully in the mind of God, then God is grossly unfair. Kind to some and unkind to others, God seems callous to human pain. Theologians try to justify how a good God can afflict us so unevenly, but their reasons wind up as "It's all a mystery." Practically speaking, if we, the handicapped, are to stay connected with God, we have to admit and express our anger. Only then will we be in a position to forgive—that last sacrifice of our egos that makes friends out of enemies.

The faith with which Matty met death, then, is no stranger to anger, but when anger is exhausted, it becomes a forgiving faith.

CHAPTER 3
The Image of God in Death

As one hand life has rendered,
The other drew death's terse sign,
A revelation in the eye's quick twinkle,
The spit and image divine.

We have looked at some of the myths in our own culture and the views in various classical sacred texts. Our purpose has been disturbance, but about a matter that warrants disturbance. While we have found problems with many of our notions about death, the one notion that remains intact for those who believe in God is that God and death are somehow connected. If this is true, then a closer look at death should tell us something more intimate about God. We are going forward on the assumption that death has never been, nor ever will be, beyond God's power. On the contrary, death is God's idea for a central, perhaps necessary, feature of the human race. We also go forward on the assumption that the ultimate reason for death lies somehow in God's loving care for us.

If all this is true, then a closer and more scrutinizing look at death will reveal to us both God and death simultaneously.

First we should recall the many other places we look for enlightenment about God—to our teachers, our sacred books, our personal experience, and to science. Taken together, they raise questions about God that we cannot easily answer. Even when we look at death, we will find that answers do not come easily, but we can at least eliminate some traditional answers that hide rather than reveal God.

Religion teachers state simple truths: God is perfect. God is love. God made everything. God is providential. God loves us. God is almighty. God sends prophets. God sent Jesus. God sends the Holy Spirit. God sent Mohammed. And on and on. But these teachings seldom complete the journey from our cool minds to our warm hearts. This God has no personality, no quirks, no face, and no history. These are ideas presented for our belief without much appeal to our experience. Learning about God in school or church is like learning about the geography of far away countries: We haven't seen these lands; we just accept what we are told as true, and it doesn't make much difference to us anyway.

People who look to the Bible to learn about God lay claim on a God with a reputation, even a gender. He has character. He has preferences. He likes the Hebrew people but not the Ammonites. He chooses the unlikely to be prophets and kings. He is patient with the hard-hearted, but only up to a point. He doesn't hesitate to entice his people's enemies into an empty tidal basin and then cover them with the sea. Unfortunately, many people who rely on the Bible, as well as people of non-Biblical religions, carry some strange ideas about this God. God is always on their side, for instance. Or God prefers to speak exclusively through church authorities. Or God thinks men make better leaders than women.

Nor does the highly personal God of the Bible square well with the terrible divine silence. It is rare that anyone who claims her "prayers were answered" experiences anything like certitude about which path to take. In any church where people are praying, all the reflection and noise are going on in the people, with nary a word from God. This "loving" God never intervenes to save a person from pain or death.

What is more, there are many believers who show the identical penchant for greed and power that nonbelievers do, and they worship this same highly personal and compassionate God. The people on both sides of wars in Israel, Iran, and Ireland—to name but a few—believe in this God of peace and reconciliation.

Besides what we have been taught, and besides what our revered religious texts say, each of us also has some Matty Ventresca in our hearts, some personal experience of God which gives still another view. God is a bright sunny day. Then God is quiet. God is moody—sometimes vibrant, sometimes boring. God is fickle, letting the wicked buy whatever they want on ill-gotten money and giving no advantage to the faithful. God will flash out in radiant smiles, plucky courage, and wacky individuality. Then God will deal out suffering in callous disregard for a person's virtue or love. God created a universe marvelous in its workings, except for the human race which forever works against its better wishes. Unexplainably, despite the bad impression God makes, people find themselves still asking God for help. They turn to God when life gets difficult. Despite their pessimism that God relieves suffering, they ask for relief anyway.

Our ideas of God have also been shaken by revelations coming from science that the universe is unimaginably vast. The awesome complexity of subatomic workings, intricately affecting the endless stretches of space with its strange black holes and quarks, at best reveal an engineering God, not an intimate friend to people in need. Our ideas have also been shaken by literary approaches to religious texts. We now regard even "sacred" texts not as plain truth but as just evidence of what some people believed. Commitment to religious truths is a more personal matter that avoids a literalist reading of "inspired" texts.

Obviously, what people *think* about God does not necessarily reveal God. In our pursuit to find God, we have no way to verify our pictures of God, some of which were painted in the oils of human selfishness. For example, isn't it true that people who pray regularly usually ask for what benefits themselves more often than for what may benefit others at their expense? Isn't it true that when we describe some event as "providential," we really mean just "good *for us*"? With death in particular, we find it difficult to reconcile the finality of loss with whatever God's so-called kind purposes might be. Does anyone normally think of death as part of God's "providence"? Like thinking about God, thinking about death can mislead us. Death may not be the worst thing that can happen to us. And, if it isn't, then *thinking* that it is may well lead us to what the worst thing really is.

So there seems to be another voice about God, a voice we do not often listen to. It is the voice of death.

True, death itself seems almost the very opposite of God. Many people take the death of a boy like Matty Ventresca as a proof that there is no God. When they reflect on Matty's suffering, beginning from his abandonment by his natural parents and continuing through his numerous illnesses until the withdrawal of life support, they see no evidence of a caring God. For them, the only possible merit of religion is functional: belief in a God tends to make some people more civil with each other, but it does not really explain anything about why Matty died and other children lived.

Yet we must admit that death and God bear a family resemblance. Neither is very impressed by us. Neither shows any respect for our schedules or for our wish to be left alone. Neither ever asks our opinion. Both death and God ridicule our efforts at getting control of our lives. These resemblances, plus the fact that we often talk about God and death in the same sentence, demonstrate the principle that life's mysteries seem to converge. Life and death, love and hate, God and evil, wisdom and foolishness, suffering and pleasure—whenever we start thinking about one of these, we end up at another. It is as if all these mysteries have a common root. At funeral parlors, during family hours, or sitting shiva, the mystery of death leads people you'd never pictured as religious to talk about God with surprising ease and familiarity—as if talk about death opened the door to their deepest religious convictions.

Likewise, people whose heart is set on God, on faith, and on loving the neighbor are not strangers to death. Their capacity for enjoying life seems in direct proportion to their capacity to endure suffering. They easily side with people on the brink of death, probably because they have sustained some kind of death to their egos. They may seem deeply centered and alive to us, but not so to themselves. They regard their center as an elusive mystery, one that requires regular dying to egotistic urges to be master of their destiny.

We need to explore, then, the connections between death and God on the assumption that death is part of God's idea of sharing divine life with us. At the same time, we should suspend belief, as far as we can, in the God we imagine. This should help us get back to the roots in our everyday experience of life and death and to approach the real God afresh.

While we suspend belief in the God we imagine, we should recall our anxieties about death. Obviously I'm assuming that despite any reassurances we have been given about the afterlife, death remains frightening for us. I expect that the answers about death already reached by civilization and handed down to us do not fully dry up our questions. Some will hesitate thinking about death because they feel it is one of the most gruesome aspects of life. This begs the question: Is it *because* we think of death as gruesome that we miss something valuable in life? If we feel that death is absolutely contrary to what is best in us, we probably overlook what really is the best in us.

No doubt, there is a risk in looking death in the face. We could become even more fearful than we already are. We might be painfully reminded of loved ones whom we still miss terribly. Still, what offense could it be to God if, in order to appreciate the gift of our lives, we take a hard look at death? Why else did God put brains in our skulls except that we might eliminate unwarranted impressions about everything in sight? And does not the death of a loved one leave the heart resolved to live more consciously in death's shadow without flinching?

To help suspend belief in the God we know, then, and to sharpen our focus on death, we will look at the following familiar images of God:

1. Is God a Creator of a World that Will End?
2. Is God a "Maker" of the World?
3. Does God Snatch Individuals from Their Families and Friends?
4. Is God All-powerful?
5. Does God Watch Us From a Distance?
6. Is God a Judge?
7. Does God Punish?
8. Is God Forgiving?

Each of these images connects to our mortality, yet upon closer examination each will prove to be illusory, and that makes all the difference in the world to what death means.

A CREATOR OF A WORLD THAT WILL END?

Matty knew that everything living eventually dies. Some things live a short life, others a long life. The fishflies that swarm in huge clouds over Higgins Lake one sticky day in July are all floating dead the next. The big elm in our front yard caught a disease and died. Aunt Nel lasted until she was ninety. But to a child like Matty, these bugs, trees, and people are "soft" things. "Hard" things like rocks and mountains seem to belong to a different realm. Being hard, they don't change. They are neither alive nor deceased. They are the solid walls, floors, and furniture for generation after generation of living things rooming there awhile.

I imagine that when Matty took Science, his eyes popped to learn that even the biggest rock on the shore is, to the geologist's eye, liquid. Like a rock of brown sugar cupped in a warm palm, it leans and sags when viewed from the long time-lines of geology. Thanks to television, we can see sped-up pictures of the earth's crust lifting and cracking like a rising angel-food cake, sinking valleys here, pushing up mountains there. Great plates that carry entire forests and seas slide by each other. In thirty-five million years, Los Angeles will be creeping by Anchorage, Alaska, heading northwest.

I don't imagine that Matty had the chance to learn about entropy, that fascinating law of universal diminishing energy. Under entropy, whenever one rock pushes another, it not only gives up kinetic energy to the other rock, making it move, it also pays an energy toll to the surroundings. Like a cosmic I.R.S., nature demands a little heat in every transfer of energy. Whenever two of its citizens make a transaction, the universe collects a tax of calories to heat up the atmosphere.

Perhaps if Matty had lived longer, he would have asked, "If that's true, then sooner or later we'll run out of energy! Everything will be just heat, and even the heat will cool off!" This is true. Great stars that warm local planets are running out of energy. Slowly, maybe, but collapsing nonetheless. The Big Dipper will eventually lose its shape and its shine.

If the entire universe of energy is collapsing, Matty might then have asked how it got so full of energy in the first place. If we are on the downside of some universal curve, what was the upside like? If it all started with a Big Bang, who packed the original explosives? So far we have no solid answers to these questions, only theories based on extrapolating data backward into unimaginable scenarios.

We live suspended between an enormous blast and a gradual decay into an everlasting dark quiet. Scientists estimate that life began 3.5 billion years ago and that the sun will bake all life to death in 1.1 billion years. We humans arrived about three-quarters into this evolutionary window of opportunity. It makes a person feel oddly lucky to have made it here while the game is still on. It also makes us wonder why we're here. If we are passing visitors on this floating raft, headed downstream toward some ultimate Falls, is there some lesson we should be learning? Did God create a world that would eventually disappear?

We cannot say what Matty may have learned from such reflections. One possible lesson is resignation. If everything eventually dies, than nothing really matters. Looking at the timeline showing the evolution of stars and of our solar system, the period in which millions upon millions of people appeared and disappeared is a tiny blip. Yet even the most rigorous scientists cannot put to rest questions about life's meaning. The heart remains disturbed by further questions, even though we can't always put those questions into words. A universe that disappears? That can't be all.

I like to think that Matty would have noticed the clue in his heart. He may have come to realize that the laws that govern the universe include the very laws that govern our wonder. The universe, after all, is everything—including these animals who raise questions, ponder, make choices, and love. The simple fact that humans everywhere dislike resignation (even though many embrace it) is clear evidence that part of the known universe is open to, seeks out, and pursues meaningful goals in the unknown part. This suggests that there may be more to life than entropy. We could look at this as just wishful thinking by optimists, but we shouldn't forget that the optimists are part of the universe too. They are plain proof that the universe also contains events in which certain beings refuse to believe that life is ultimately meaningless. One only has to examine any point in the universe at which acts of reflection occur. There, one usually finds refusals to give up occurring too.

Something deep within us expects that our individual lives have a meaning that death cannot eliminate. Certainly, much of that meaning will be remembered and carried on by our survivors. Our children carry on our name and style. Our friends call us to mind and tell stories about us. But the meaning of our lives is not confined to the stories people tell. More often than not, the stories oversimplify the original meaning of what we were up to anyway. Original meaning has a reality of its own. When a woman drops a five-dollar bill into the hat of a blind beggar, no one but herself may ever know the story, but she parts with her money because it has a meaning that is real. It cannot be eliminated by revisionist interpretations. Its meaning is immortal. It matters.

Newton reflected on the falling apple and concluded that a Law of Gravity pervades the universe. In the same way, reflecting on the phenomenon of human hope in the permanence of meaning, we can conclude that besides the law of entropy, there is another law at work, a law just as real and effective as any law of physics. (We will look more closely at this law in the next chapter.)

Everything still dies. But the presence of hope in billions of hearts is a raft of data that begs explanation. The least we can say is that death does not always mean complete annihilation. Hope is a real event experienced by everyone, an event regarded everywhere as a key to something bigger than death. Perhaps some of this world will end, but there are rumblings that not everything ends. And despite the fact that Matty probably did not think much about cosmology, if through some miracle he had lived long enough, I'd bet his sense of hope would have outdistanced most of ours.

MAKER OF THE WORLD?

Mention of entropy brings to mind old debates on creation and evolution. Every once in a while, we hear of God-fearing folks chastising yet another high school science teacher for teaching "evolution" to their children. Just as often, other teachers enrage the secularly enlightened folks for teaching "creationism" to *their* children.

Although the debate is on how humans began, it also affects our view of how humans end. To the evolutionist, the death of an individual is a necessary part of a natural process whereby early forms give way to later, and possibly higher, forms. Early forms have to get out of the way, so to speak, sometimes to make room for later forms and sometimes to give up control of local resources on which higher forms depend. But evolution seems to have no ultimate end, only successively higher ends, and, when local environments can no longer support whatever forms have emerged, then *that's* the "end" of them. When our planetary biosphere can no longer sustain us, that will be the end of us too. To the evolutionist, our "end" is about time, not purpose.

To the creationist, the death of individuals is the beginning of a new and higher life. God lifts us off the earth in a reversal of the process by which we were first set down here. The evolutionist view answers quite a different question than the creationist view because, for the creationist, the "end" of human life is about purpose, not time. Human manipulation of ends and means should therefore be carried out with our ultimate end in mind. Having an end in the next life means we do not really "end" at our death in this one.

The media usually describe these disputes as clashes between science and religion. They set up the question as a debate between two beliefs: either Creationists are wrong and Evolutionists are right, so that death is just a biological endpoint—or vice-versa, making death only a step in a journey to an endpoint in a higher life. I would like to make the case that neither alternative is true. These rather are clashes between two parties who misunderstand both science and religion.

Any intelligent approach must start with the fact that this death that we seek to understand is a single reality, but that we can ask about it from different perspectives. So theology asks one kind of question and science asks another. But like everything we study, our different angles of approach ought to converge. It should be possible to understand death in a way that contradicts neither science nor religion. One very fruitful way of avoiding contradictions is to start by seeing how the mind works to create knowledge. There are many differences between science and religion, of course, but a major difference lies in the kind of knowledge each discipline aims to convey, a difference that we can abbreviate with the words *whether* and *how*.

The religious doctrine that God created us is a *whether* statement. The question that resulted in the doctrine is this: Is God responsible for humanity or not? The answer is either a Yes or a No. It is either an affirmation or a negation. The realities that are the focus of specifically religious belief are just too mysterious for anyone to make dogmatic statements about *how* God went about creating. The accounts of creation in practically every religion were understood even to their original audiences as metaphorical narratives aimed to answer the question *whether* or not God is behind it all. In *Genesis*, for example, the stories were likely written to counteract other creation stories then current that gave the credit to sex or the snake and made gods out of them. Although the use of a narrative form required descriptions of creation taking place, the purpose of the stories was to state *whether* God accomplished it, not *how*.

Science teachers who believe that humans evolved from apes are making *how* statements. Their guiding question is: How did human beings come to be? Explain the process, please. It is beyond the realm of science to make dogmatic statements about *whether* God is the ultimate origin of things. Scientific method does not aim for final certitudes; it aims for best available explanations. And explanations are quite a different matter than simple true/false statements.

Still, science and religion are essentially two realms of questions in the human mind. Only as a result of these two realms in the mind do we find, on the one hand, collections of labs, chemicals, instruments, and researchers and, on the other, churches, prayer books, candles, and incense. So the creationist has every right to ask a scientific question. Indeed, the idea that creation might be a little complicated ought to make a creationist *more* impressed with God, not less. If we imagine that God creates everything through the instrumentality of probabilities and that the inventiveness of humans (we who likewise arrived according to the workings of probabilities) is part of God's way of creating, should we be scandalized? Must we defend the story that God placed us one-by-one on earth as a child sets dolls on an imaginary stage? Does it increase our reverence for the mystery of creation if we insist God must be simple-minded?

By the same token, the scientist cannot help but ask the question about the meaning of death and to find clues in the way things in the world die. Science in its own right, after all, presumes a view of nature that repudiates the idea that death is an annihilation. The notion that death is a total end is a completely foreign exception to how the universe runs. That is, although it is not the business of science to make *whether* statements about our ultimate origins and destiny, science gives evidence everywhere that death is not an end. The theory of evolution actually reinforces the idea that, wherever death occurs, higher life emerges.

For example, when we look at the destiny of things, everything "dies" in service to some bigger thing. Free electrons "die" when captured by an atom. Atoms are constrained when chained into molecules. Molecules serve chemical rulers. Nervous systems in clams obey the dictates of their sensitive systems. A raccoon's sensitive system is subordinate to its mating instincts. In humans, ideas are incorporated into decisions, decisions into action, action into results. People belong to communities. Communities belong to history. What, then, is the larger, directive system after history? Science will not make any pronouncements here because the evidence is not conclusive and probably never will be. But if there is any universal pattern in the universe that science reveals, it is clear that destiny everywhere involves a kind of death, not a death by annihilation but a death by an incorporation.

Likewise, when we look at the origin of things, everything comes from earlier things. Planets came from astral debris. Rocks come from hot magma. Apples from seeds. Fawns from deer. Today's weather from yesterday's. You and I from our parents. Social institutions from plans, plans from insights, insights from wonder. But to accomplish this, nature slaughters with mindless abandon. Most bright ideas are killed under the scrutiny of verification. Every year the maple tree in our backyard sends thousands of little helicopters spinning down to the lawn, all destined to rot or to sprout shoots sliced off by my lawnmower. Tens of millions of a man's sperm swarm around a woman's egg on the chance that one might fertilize, with the rest returning to the ecosystem, their highest potential now dead. The Big Bang that established the architecture of the known universe five billion years ago was itself one probability among many that never came to be. What alternative universes might there have been? Would they be governed by gravity, electromagnetism, strong and weak atomic glue? We cannot say. But here again the rule seems to be that every mortal thing is born from a prior mortal thing, and that billions of potential forms die for every form that is actualized. Clearly, the ultimate origin of the universe contains mortality in some fashion.

Both the origin and the destiny of the human universe are indescribable. And they always will be because we are speaking of a level of being quite beyond our own. We are fish talking about air. We could no more give accurate descriptions of this larger view than cats could tell jokes.

Yet cats thrive within a larger, human world. (Indeed, were cats equipped with the appropriate wonder, they would be insulted over the many jokes told at their expense!) We too live in a world larger than we can describe, a world whose origin and destiny affect our everyday lives in ways beyond our comprehension. Maybe celestial beings are falling over, laughing over jokes about us, just as we do about our cats. Or maybe there are no celestial beings, only God. We can't really say. However, unlike cats, at least we have the appropriate wonder. Nothing else in the universe we know about can wonder, and wonder is the power to question everything. In particular, we bear the unsettling questions about our origin and destiny. This is why our lives are mysterious to us while life to a cat is no mystery at all, just a series of nips and naps and lion practice.

So both creation and evolution are mysterious. Neither is a set of unambiguous teachings that should command the loyalty of zealous groups. And a mystery is a reality we continuously question without ever getting certitude, a reality that bothers us, that draws us to itself through the services of a wonder in us that won't stop. Death is such a mystery. We don't completely understand it, yet to it we are drawn.

Indeed, isn't everything we experience a mystery? No matter how familiar things are, the fact that they are simply *there* has seized the attention of poets and artists everywhere. We cannot help but marvel at the fact that we exist, when we know very well that we did not have to be. And God, thought of as the ultimate origin and destiny of everything, is the ultimate mystery. Not the ultimately unknowable God of agnostics, whose sense of the divine runs so deep they resist taking the very non-logical step to believing that this rampant inner wonder is Someone's gift. No, when we say God is the ultimate mystery, we are saying that we cannot reach God by certitudes, only by faith. If we ever reach a demonstrable certainty about God, we should worry.

By saying that God is the ultimate mystery, we are also saying that whenever we wonder, it may well be by God's thread tugging our hearts and minds. This mysterious behind and beyond surrounds us, infuses every thought, every feeling. Everything that is so familiar to us is mostly beyond our comprehension. Certainly we ought to spell out religious doctrines, but more as fences to corral religiously fanatical thinking than as clear disclosures about the divine. And certainly we should continue explaining how the world evolves, but more as plausible explanations that will give way to later explanations that make more sense. While all this is going on, though, it remains extremely important to use the mind simply to acknowledge and reverence the ultimate mystery of the universe and its divine origins and destiny. It is the kind of thinking one does sitting quietly on a hill somewhere, remembering how answerless our wonder is. It is contemplation.

In such a contemplation we make simple affirmations. We look at aspects of the human condition and point in the direction of God to indicate their sources and destinies.

So let me offer a few short philosophical koans that may help keep our minds focused on the mystery. I recommend these for contemplation. You will recall that contemplation has to be kept simple. This involves suppressing questions of why these statements may be true, or how they work out in practice. It also means suppressing your imagination (artists in particular will want to portray these somehow). Even suppress your feelings; neither let your possibilities excite you nor your failures depress you. Just acknowledge that these statements are true. Just say Yes:

> Whatever beauty we appreciate, it is beautiful by a beauty-full God. Wherever we, like God, make beauty, we too are beautiful, made so by the artistry of God.
>
> Whatever design we find, it is designed by the design of God. Whatever we, like God, design, we too are designed, a design made intelligently by God.
>
> Whatever we say is so, it is so by the say-so of God. Whenever we, like God, make something so, we too are so, made so by the Yes of God.
>
> Whatever we find good, it is good by the goodness of God. Whenever we, like God, make good, we too are good, made good by the kindness of God.
>
> Whomever we love are lovable by the love of God. Whenever we, like God, make love, we too are lovable, made so by the passion of God.

MY INDIVIDUAL SAVIOR?

From what we have said thus far, we have evidence, though not proof, that something about life is immortal and that any really satisfying immortality is not just endless life. The presence of human hope in the face of disasters and the recurrence of human wonder despite confusion about creation and evolution point to the divine. The deathless prize we yearn for lies in making something meaningful of ourselves and creating meaningful ties to others. So, even though everything we know of comes to an end, there is still a wonderful and mysterious kind of eternity in the natural universe. It can be found in human hearts, in the way our consciences and understanding reach out beyond death.

Isn't this rather subtle, though? Isn't it far easier to believe in an afterlife, where we carry on and where our good deeds are rewarded and bad deeds punished? Philosophical arguments that prove there is a life after this one do not exactly knock the wind out of us. In any case, most people who believe in an afterlife inherited that belief without much question. And many of those who later examined this belief closely rejected it as wishful thinking or as a myth suitable for children only.

If we suppose, for a moment, that belief in an afterlife is a mistake, with no foundation in reality, then we are brought back to wondering what kind of immortality lies on this side of the grave. We can find that immortality by looking at how all of us are somehow tied into the human family. That immortality can be seen in how we make life "civil."

Civilizations are the result of events in which humans reached out for what endures and were doing so consciously. The millions of decisions made over the centuries by men and women seeing permanent worth in following certain courses of action have played an essential part in the evolution of all human communities. Despite the wars and the callous use of people as if they were disposable pens, people of genuine hope have everywhere conducted themselves with compassion, self-sacrifice, and an intelligence that sets common good over personal gain. They do not want their contribution to die. They want to leave an immortal mark on the world. We do not easily notice this because most people seek this immortality quietly. While accounts of wars are easy stuff for historians because the data is public, much more difficult are accounts of how the hope of billions of anonymous people has contributed to civilization. Any easy dismissal of that contribution to the benefit of humankind overlooks the vast majority of events on which all genuine progress to date has depended.

It is rather easy to see this "immortality" in the way groups carry on despite the death of their members. Look at the rest of nature, where the death of individual things becomes the life of larger things. Forests last for centuries because the old trees drop seeds and fall out of the way for seedlings to replace them. Among animals, that larger "thing" is a hive, a herd, a swarm. Among us rational animals, that bigger "thing" is community, togetherness, friendship, the universal network of love and caring that links one person to another.

Also, a look at the exact manner in which the individual death of a human draws meaning from the larger community reveals some interesting aspects about death. Is it not true that we become our best selves when we engage our lives with others? Is it not a universal experience that when we exchange energy with others, we are much more "alive" than if we hoard what we have? Is it not true even about our garbage insofar as we return our leftovers to the land with a mind to its replenishment? Yet is it not also a fact that in every such life-giving exchange, we "die" a little? Every time we yield some privilege or give up some possession to others, we are also giving up—letting die—a potential self that we are capable of becoming. In other words, the larger reality of human community thrives precisely to the extent that its members "die" in some fashion.

This gives us a somewhat larger view of the total picture. Although entropy continues to erode the foundations of the physical world, spirit is busy building on new footings. Although every human will die, communities carry on. Some might object that communities themselves die, but the death of communities is nothing like the death of the individual. In the "death" of most communities, the last members move on to other communities, carrying with them much of the cultural wisdom and practical lore of the "dead" community. Families do not exactly "die." Members are born and members die, but, if all the data were available, we could weave a string of stories where each chapter depended on the previous and set the stage for the next as one family proliferates into others with very different names.

What exactly is it that a community "carries on" beyond the deaths of its members and through its various transformations? It is neither the group's name, nor its property, nor even necessarily its bloodline that carries on. What makes a community a community is shared meaning—its ways of life, its priorities, its language, its protocols, its laws, its ethics, its art, every single insight that shaped the ways it circulates money, fuel, and the news of the day. Each such element of meaning originated through the creativity of some member, a member who dies while the contribution carries on.

In the long course of history, this work of carrying on the values and meanings of a community has been looked at in two mutually-opposed ways, which we might call the Originalist and the Progressive.

Most of our distant ancestors were Originalist. They never imagined that the human spirit had the creativity capable of improving our life together. Older philosophers and historians believed that a civilization improved only to the extent that it returned to the original wisdom of the ancients. We can still hear echoes of this conviction in the common wisdom among many older people everywhere that the past was better than the present. Even the great story of creation in Genesis and its variant in the Koran depict us as off to a great start and then tripping up by an "original" sin. Politicians and educators concluded that civilized life is something to be kept in good repair against the storms of barbarian invasion and natural disasters. To shore up a culture, leaders used planks inherited from forebears. What counted was memory, not creativity.

But since the arrival of empirical science and the philosophical reflections of August Comte and Karl Marx, people in developed countries now think of the human vocation as a matter of progress and invention. In this Progressive view, we are called to *improve* the human condition, which means to surpass the wisdom of the ancients. We do not wrap ourselves in our origins; we stand upon them and build from there. Nowadays, no one can read a history book without the background notion that even the worst wars are only temporary setbacks to a natural progression of history into something better.

Parents, for example, typically forgo their own satisfactions to make things better for their children. Many an aging mother has been laid to rest with the comforting thought that at least she gave her kids a chance at a better life than she had. And *her* kids will feel the same about their kids. During an economic recession, we hold our breath, waiting for the market to find itself again, as if it somehow must. In developed countries, people carry a deep confidence that the economy somewhat naturally expands, eventually delivers ever higher returns, and improves the general standard of living in the long run.

Strict Originalist thinking seems too short-sighted to most people. It tends to suppress change and to devalue adaptation to changing circumstances. Yet strict Progressivist thinking tends to be too far-sighted insofar as it presumes that history practically improves itself. Progressivists fixate on a wonderful future that, somehow, will automatically emerge, as if our planet were some kind of egg with a marvelous chicken inside. You would think that genocide, racial vengeance, and anti-government terrorism—the particular horrors of our times—would have tempered any belief that this progress should be automatic.

Still, I see the scales of history as tipped a little to the Progressive side—not automatic, but progressing on account of a dynamism in nature that, statistically speaking, tends to hit on the improved form, the better configuration, the optimal integration of materials. Many people will dispute the existence of such a dynamism. They feel that the Natural Selection is sufficient to explain how higher entities emerge from lower ones. That is, they subscribe to the idea that as chance genetic variations give certain plants and animals an advantage, these tend to reproduce, while those without this genetic edge simple don't survive.

But this doesn't explain the phenomenal organization of plants and animals everywhere. Who, watching Saturday-afternoon nature programs on TV, can help but marvel at the complex yet economical way that the simplest organisms evolve, how cellular life yields control to conscious life and animal sensitivity, and how that animal sensitivity is only a jumping-off platform for the magnificent leap to intelligence in humans? Scientists who believe that the law of natural selection sufficiently explains the emergence of forms that are more adaptable to alien surroundings usually overlook the fact that once new forms arrive on the evolutionary stage, they take charge of all the stagehands and props, making it *less* likely that they will be replaced by yet higher forms. Other scientists, however, based on this evidence alone, propose that there must be another law at work in nature besides natural selection. This other law predisposes matter not merely to forms more adaptive to surroundings but forms of successively higher centralized control. This law may not guarantee progressive evolution at every step, but neither is evolution controlled merely by genetic accidents hitting on mutations that are better equipped to survive.

The evidence of such a law of emerging spirit explains the emergence not only of human individuals but of human communities making meaning in history. And because it does so, it gives our hope in immortality some this-worldly objectivity. In other words, despite the common belief that God saves individuals while communities become irrelevant, there is no individual immortality without a communal immortality. Of course we must understand this immortality as residing in the realm of *meaning*, not in the realm of *time*. We must look for the meaning of any one person's life chiefly in his or her contribution to the commonweal. This is the contribution that becomes irreversible—immortal—at one's death.

Think again of Matty Ventresca and you cannot help but think of Gina, Brian, and Kimy as well. Does anyone doubt that Matty's cheerfulness came from his family? Is anyone surprised that Matty's courage was inherited from spouses who adopted a handicapped child? These are the meanings that are immortal. The "Matty" died, but the "Ventresca" lives. At the human level, evolution occurs in the realm of virtues rather than biological substrata. New species of care regularly spring up, usually under the action of forgiveness.

The idea that God somehow "removed" Matty from earthly things simply misses what Matty *means* to his family, to me, and perhaps now to you, the reader. The same is true for anyone who dies. To imagine that God lifted him away, like removing a card from a deck, overlooks the fact that the world today bears Matty's remains, not just in the earth, but in the minds and hearts of all who knew him.

AN ALL-POWERFUL GOD?

I do not know Matty's frailty. I never suffered the kind of diseases he did. Once, during my bout with cancer, I thought I could approximate the day of my death, and so for a brief few weeks savored the gift of each day, much as Matty did. But the scare passed and I returned to normal life feeling rather strong and on top of things.

Recently, though, a sense of frailty is returning. I would like to describe it, partly because I'm beginning to understand Matty's view of life, and partly because I have discovered that in the experience of frailty God touches us in a very intimate way.

My growing sense of frailty comes with aging. I'm getting up there. Getting on in years. When I think about the end, it seems to be far away. But when, after not thinking about it for a few months, I look at it again, it seems a little closer, like bush-covered aborigines sneaking up on cattle, spears poised.

Although the end approaches imperceptibly, I feel its pressure on me to choose between possibilities. When I was eighteen years old, so many possibilities surrounded me that I didn't really have to decide. I more or less fell into things—these friends, this school, and these hobbies. But recently I've begun to watch my step. Every choice *for* is also a choice *against*. I think that I could learn to play the clarinet, and I would like to. But I doubt that I will because there are other things I would like to do, and time is running out.

Despite actuaries telling me that my chances of not seeing seventy are about 25 percent, I'm confident I'll be able to choose a few more things to do before the end. Perhaps my confidence stems from comparing myself to people older or more infirm, for whom options have already run out. There is very little for them to do. People turn down their offers to help. Each day, time embezzles a little from their bank of helpful energy. Each month erodes their dexterity and renders them less helpful. Many younger people really do not want the help of their elders because they prefer speed and zest to deliberation and care.

Modern medicine has made old age more possible for almost everyone. Not everyone is cheering, however. One is forced to retire from everyday employment. One's life changes dramatically. On numerous fronts, one has to begin a new life. Maybe it's a life lived at home, maybe a life of travel, maybe a life spent learning new skills and working on neglected hobbies. Most likely it will be a life increasingly dedicated to health maintenance. But all this requires dedication, discipline, and encouragement from others if old age is to be anything but a boring wait out here in life's right field for the big pop fly.

Old people want to be useful. Usefulness is the yardstick that measures the quality of their lives. Of course, younger idealists will insist that there is more to life than usefulness. They protest being forced into situations in which they might "be used." But being used is enough for the elderly. My mother-in-law comes into the kitchen and asks, "Can I do anything?" And, with superfluous good will but abysmal understanding, we tell her, "No, Mom. You can just sit down and relax." But she doesn't want to relax. Her bones know that relaxation is a step away from death, and she still feels in those bones the ability to help others.

It takes years to really like the idea of being useful. Children balk at being more useful around the house. To them, being useful is an unwelcome interruption to play. Even as adults, being useful is usually a means to other ends. It gains you esteem, job promotion, power, perhaps love. To the elderly, however, being useful is just that, simply being of some use for someone else. No rewards or punishments. Winning the esteem and love of others has become unimportant. What's important is to be able to give. True, this generosity may be driven partly by raw fear of being cast aside, yet even that is as much fear of the meaninglessness of an unshared life as it is fear of rejection.

There may be senior citizens fully dedicated to doing nothing, but I've never met one. Seniors either show remarkable zest for what's new or, if they are handicapped by diminishing capacities, show open resentment that they can't put their desires into action. So, "the spirit is willing but the flesh is weak." The Christian apostle Paul wrote that wonderful phrase to sum up the difficulty of avoiding sin. But it applies in spades to getting old. It seems the older we get, as our spirit more urgently insists on staying involved, our flesh more stubbornly refuses to cooperate. Everyone who does not die young faces this anomaly.

It is easy to resent this aspect of the human condition. But resentment gets old too. Sooner or later we find ourselves wondering whether resentment is really appropriate. If this simultaneous expansion of the spirit and contraction of the means to put its inspirations into practice are part of the human condition, part of human nature that is not exclusively about evil, then there may be something good in it. There may be some value in being weak.

Again, Paul: "My power is at its best in weakness." We need to face the possibility that God's involvement with humanity *necessarily* brings weakness with it. That is, deep in God's character, there may be a kind of frailty that has eternal worth. The weakness of the flesh, while it surely accounts for malice in the world, may also tell us something about God.

God works best against odds, it seems. Human life is meant to be a struggle, not a perpetual escape from struggle. It is God's wisdom that designed the human condition to involve putting things together and repairing what's broken. We create, we rest. We rest, there's trouble. We fix the problem or redeem the situation, we rest. Trouble again. By the time we're old, we are leery of rest. We imagine "rest homes" as the worst fate awaiting us, our blood laced with Haldol, our minds turned to mayonnaise.

Gradually it comes clear that God doesn't simply *create* life. God holds life for those who will fight for it. This is a clear reflection of God's feisty and restless personality. "I will give you your life as a prize of war," God says to Baruch. Does God require human struggle because of human sin? Perhaps. Still, the idea that God rests in absolute peace while we drive each other crazy does not square with the belief of most people that God loves us. Take *that* idea, and develop it, and you end up with the possibility that in human suffering God may be sharing something absolutely personal and divine with us. They say doctors play God, but not this God. That God is aloof, capricious, antiseptic, and comfortable. This God is involved, loyal, dirty, and restless. That God sends patients home. This God comes home with the patient.

So maybe getting old means drawing closer and closer to God's frail center. Perhaps the unfairness of waxing in wisdom while waning in strength is only apparent. Age's cruel agonies may not be evil. While we shouldn't go so far as to say that aging is better for us, neither should we say it makes us worse persons. We fight to the end. Even when we stop fighting in our conscious minds, our hearts stubbornly keep pumping, our chests heaving, until the last cells finally yield. It would not be appropriate to compare this struggle to a wrestling match, where the point is to win. Here the point is just to wrestle. The "life" that is a prize of war is *not* one that simply goes on. Real "life," mysterious though it be, is something that *includes* getting older and feebler, enduring the slow losses one by one.

We can look at frailty from another angle. A traditional spirituality counts frailty as a letting go of all the temporary supports to our sense of self and allowing God to take us, dispossessed and nervous, to divine beatitude. Frailty is a reminder that we are not God; we are human. The trouble with this view is that it discounts all the creaturely things we touched and loved. It belittles the millions of ways in which we depended on God's creation. It portrays God as having all the power, stubbornly holding it all, and refusing to let anyone approach unless they're stripped of every possession. It portrays God as liking us, but on condition that we don't like anything else. "You can't take it with you," the adage says.

I, for one, don't believe it. You *can* take it with you. I believe that those who live authentic lives will lose nothing of any thing or any person affected by them. I look at it this way: At my death, even should I find no physical comfort or emotional consolation, I hope that faith will assure me that nothing worthwhile shall be lost. I hope that God is interested not just in me but in my company, my friends, my acquaintances, in everyone whose life I may have touched. I want to "take with me" anything that I shared with others. God's original idea of me, after all, resulted first from the grand idea of a human family making history. So it seems appropriate to think of God not simply as removing me from my surroundings but rather as improving my surroundings by the way I die. From God's point of view, my death is an act of a community living on in history.

So too for every individual's death. Each death is the Kingdom coming, part of the divine process of sharing life. Far from receiving power from God, death is receiving an exquisite vulnerability from God.

You'll remind me, though? I'll probably forget.

A GOD WATCHING FROM A DISTANCE?

Imagine yourself, at five years old, being told that you are very special. And the reason you are special is that you will never see high school. You will die first. Matty Ventresca's response to this news was fearless, owing to how his parents told him and perhaps to a natural fearlessness in children about death. Still, whether Matty had to live his few years in fear or in hope, he had to live in the shadow of a mortal deadline.

We all live in this shadow to some extent. We know we will die someday. We hope to get our families raised and some projects completed. Because we don't think about our death much, you would think we would act as though life might continue forever. This is hardly the case. We act as though there never is enough time. The hands of our clocks point accusingly. Their faces stare out impatiently. Yet we seem to like their scolding presence. We wear clocks on our wrists: we call them "watches" as if they have been appointed to remind us of our duties. We hang clocks all over the house. In the kitchen especially: our kitchen has a clock on the stove, a clock on the microwave, a clock on the coffee maker, and, in a space of honor by itself, a clock on the wall. We have two calendars on the refrigerator, along with half a dozen yellow sticky notes. We even have a sundial on our garage. We are being watched, reminded, beckoned. We dream for the day when we can live without their tyranny.

That day comes when we retire. Then we discover too late that we don't know what to do with ourselves. Our "natural" self—that imaginary Robinson Crusoe liberated from the chains of an overscheduled civilization—is bored cross-eyed. So we set a date with friends—"Meet you at 7:30." We join a volunteer group, which expects us to be there Saturday morning, 9 o'clock, sharp. Our hoped-for escape from timetables turned out to be a disaster. We quickly get on the phone with calendar in hand.

So clocks and schedules have their place. They belong among our instruments for staying connected. Dates are really about staying plugged to the pipelines of life. Not only the "dates" we go on when we're single, but all the dates we set with other people. Meeting together for business is the human way of making sure that people are well served somehow. Hardly romantic, meeting to serve others is an act of love.

It is important not to name time as our enemy, lest we overlook what really threatens human life. Time can be a framework for love and care. Our schedules, appointments, and dates are the only way we know how to make our benevolence work. They are the means by which we stay connected to each other. They can give us the opportunity to rely on others in our needs and to allow others to rely on us.

Unfortunately, these schedules, appointments, and dates can also be hate channels. People plot to undo others, using clocks and calendars to ensure efficiency. But time is not the enemy here, either. The enemy is something that twists the heart, and a twisted heart is the major, if not exclusive, enemy of our natural vocation. Time, far from being our enemy, is the victim of our true enemy.

What is God's idea of time? In our imagination, we tend to think of absolutely everything as bound by and living in time. Yet philosophical reflection usually concludes that God is beyond time; God invented time. But what is behind God's idea of time? If God made time for some purpose, what might that purpose be?

We must think in metaphors here. The easy metaphor is that life is a game whose end is set like an alarm on a clock. Our experiences as children teach us that we have only a limited time to do the chores assigned by our parents. What counts is not what we are doing at this minute but what we will have done when the time is up. We idealize the deathbed conversion, as if that moment were the most important moment in our lives. As we grow up, however, that simplistic view loosens its hold on our spiritual imagination. The significance of time is not to set a day of reckoning.

Nor do we have to look back to the beginning of time to understand God's purpose. We can see a purpose to God's idea of time by looking at how God creates in the present. In our various reflections above we noted that God's habit is to *build* life, not create it full flower out of nothing. God works slowly, not suddenly. And God works through the working of the universe itself. That is, God does not create new-minted coins to slot into the world as it is. Instead, God has charged the world as it is with an energy that brings forth new forms according to its own ancient laws. Certainly the slow evolution of planets and of civilization on this planet gives us reason to respect God's patient way of bringing forth life. In this perspective, God's idea of time was to make it possible for us to collaborate with the divine. Time is divine room to make mistakes as we grope our way through life. Time tilts the odds to our side that we will find God and allow God to work in us.

With human life in particular, God seems to loathe acting independently of us. There is no unquestionable miracle, recorded by any religion, that God has ever performed without time-consuming human cooperation. In other words, it seems that God wants to build life *with* us on earth, not just *for* us on some land beyond.

This patient and gradual nature of divine collaboration runs extremely deep. For example, look at how each one of us collaborates with God as our minds evolve. As children we depended on images. In grade schools we developed our understanding and in high school the ability and intention to verify our beliefs. We are not alone in this development. We are engaged with God as our free choices interact with God's inspirations. This takes time, and this takes care. This takes community, and this takes history.

Still, community and history have never been universally popular among the people responsible for creating community and whose mistakes make history. Jean-Paul Sartre's *No Exit,* proposes that "Hell is other people." Margaret Thatcher once said, "There is no such thing as society. There are only men and women and their families." And many honorable thinkers regard history as nothing but illusion, that nothing really "goes forward." For example, Ralph Waldo Emerson: "There is properly no history; only biography." But for people who believe that God has fully shared the divine life with us, creating us in the divine image and likeness, it means that there is something about community and history that lies at the heart of the divine essence.

I find it interesting that nothing in any religious tradition prevents us from believing that God may have created another solar system to share divine life with other creatures. Suppose there is intelligent life out there. If their spiritual features have really been drawn from God's most intimate self, then they would absolutely have to be creatures working out their life together over time. Contrary to what some science-fiction movies depict, there would not be a race of pure, unfailing minds, living in perfect harmony with the natural universe. In some respect it would be hearts and minds dealing with each other, needing forgiveness as much as love, subject to death like us, and going to that death with hope for their posterity. Because they too will weave their destinies from a beginning to an end, shuttling from solitariness to community and back, they will need watches to help them watch out. I can see no other conclusion if our condition of living in community and history are an essential share in the divine life of God.

A JUDGE?

When I was young, I was taught that many things were wrong: murder, stealing, lying, taking God's name in vain, fornication, birth control, abortion, etc. This was *The List*. Do them and you did wrong.

Morality had an immediate connection to death. Do wrong and you suffer in the next life. Death was simply one's last chance to do something right and to repent of all the wrong things. We were encouraged to pray for the grace of having time for a deathbed confession. In the *Hail Mary*, we Catholics asked Mary to "pray for us sinners now and at the hour of our death."

Then came sophomore year high school, when this simple framework became unglued. The great enterprise was to exasperate teachers by thinking up exceptions to rules. You could legitimately murder in a war. A desperately hungry person could steal food. You could lie to people who had no right to know what you know. You could even fornicate if you were stranded for years on a deserted island with someone of the opposite sex and had no hope of ever seeing anyone from civilization again. (Sophomore year, remember.)

Because I was raised in a strict Catholic environment, birth control and abortion stayed clearly wrong without exceptions. Ironically, despite our wild attacks on The List, no one questioned that The List existed, mostly in the minds of parents and certainly in the mind of God. The basic myth was still complete. We had swallowed it hook, line, and sinker, reel, creel, and boat.

But gradually I began to make moral judgments about matters not on The List. Being inconsiderate of others began to feel wrong. Carelessness about my health, taking stupid risks in the car, ignoring small inspirations to say a kind word—experiences like these nagged my conscience.

At the same time I began to do some of the forbidden things on The List because, at the time, I didn't know what else to do. I'd lie to my parents simply because I didn't know how to tell adults courteously to mind their own business. I explored sexuality in a manner that certainly violated the bounds of intimacy and respect taught me by my religion, yet to this day I cannot envision how I reached what meager maturity I may have without those "mistakes."

The transition from belief in a List to a fundamental trust in conscience was prolonged and difficult. I was *taught* to trust the word of authority; but I had to learn on my own to transfer that trust to my conscience. The word of authority in my early days cautioned me against the evils of everyone deciding privately what's right and wrong. Catholic authorities in particular emphasized the dangers of "private inspiration." These were the terrible mistakes, I was told, that made Protestant churches continually subdivide in history. Yet my conscience gradually grew more intelligent and more insistent on taking charge.

What eased the transition was a conviction that God is kind. God's kindness, in turn, was measured by my experience of the kindness of my parents. My parents made it clear that they wanted me to take responsibility for what I thought and what I did. The List, like my parents' rule about looking both ways before crossing the street, was just a provisional introduction to growing up.

Some good schooling helped too. In History class I learned that charging interest on a loan was considered wrong only during certain historical periods. In Religion I learned that no one in New Testament times thought capital punishment might be wrong; not even Jesus denounced the practice. Eventually I had to endure the moral shock of realizing that every moral rule sprung from ordinary people like me trying to make sense out of their experience.

There was no permanent, immutable List.

The shock reverberated through everything spiritual in me. The entire task of life turned out to be something very different than behaving properly and avoiding penalties. You had to act responsibly. This meant following your conscience and using your head. You had to be intelligent about figuring out good and bad. You relied on traditional values and codes of conduct for the most part and, in situations that presented real moral dilemmas, you used the head you happened to have and did your best.

St. Thomas Aquinas probably went through the same hesitation before putting conscience above law. But his mind was eventually clear on the matter: "Better to die excommunicated than to violate our conscience," he said.

The effect of debunking The List, far from freeing me to act in any way I pleased, instead made me face up to the thousands of times I neglected to carry through on good ideas. Standing before a kindly God, not an Accountant in the sky, I became more the sinner. More the sinner, not by doing more Wrong Things but by seeing all the wrong things I had always been doing and still doing them. I may be presumptuous here, but I believe I understand what the saints meant when, fully intending to state the absolute truth, they claimed to be great sinners, sinning even while standing in God's great shower of grace. Their sins, like mine, were 90 percent failures to obey inspirations to offer someone a hand or suppress a sarcastic remark. When one realizes that inspirations are God's work on our behalf, every inner disobedience tells God, "You're wasting your time; stop bothering me."

Where I formerly had divided life into three parts—good deeds, bad deeds, and a huge middle part labeled "neutral"—I gradually saw there is no middle. Everything is grace or sin. In this revelation, I was fortunate to be thoroughly immersed in a theology of history taught by Ignatius Loyola. From his "Two Standards" meditation I learned that the heart is a battleground of two subtle but opposed forces. A gentle voice usually draws us to the ungarnished truth and to looking for what is objectively the best, not what pays off just for us. A more agitated voice usually yanks us toward securing a place for ourselves and muscling others out of our way. Every inclination, every impulse, every thought and emotion occurs on this moral slope leading either upward toward grace or downward toward sin. There simply is no neutral event that does not somehow enter into our making of ourselves what we are becoming.

This moral shock of realizing that all we poor humans have is our minds and consciences doesn't eliminate The List in one's mind overnight. If my experience is common and I may speak for all, even after we have seen how conscience and understanding are the sources of everything we call "good," we spontaneously consult The List to judge others, to scold them, to dismiss them. We use The List as a moral bludgeon. It is habitual, and it is also far easier than trying to understand every situation we run into.

What is more serious, The List seduces us with a tempting offer of power over others. Parents easily lord it over their children. When they say "That's good" or "That's bad," without ever appealing to their children's understanding, they poison the normal growth of young consciences and probably harden their own.

Relying on conscience and intelligence may well be described as a "situation ethics." By that I do not mean the approach that discounts practically everything in tradition in an attempt to look at a situation with a fresh mind. That kind of situation ethics is naïve. A "fresh" mind is not an empty mind. I believe a good juror is someone who knows a lot about the situation, even though some of that knowledge may be incorrect. I'd much rather rely on the mind's ability to raise a relevant question, an ability which only familiarity can give, than on a mind free of all bias because it has never thought about the matter at hand. In the same way, the best moral mind is the mind that knows some history and can reasonably consider moral judgments made in the past and adapt them to the present situation.

The "situation" I have in mind here includes everything anyone involved already knows and everything they can ask about. That is, the situation always includes the *mindsets* of the participants. It includes the values passed on by tradition. It also includes the practical experience and judgment of the people involved as they adjust their scale of moral priorities in the face of new problems.

A few years ago Catholic officials illustrated the wisdom of adapting past practices and values to a present, unforeseen situation. At the 1994 United Nations Population Conference in Cairo, the Vatican decided not to object to clear assumptions that artificial birth control would be the preferred means of restraining population growth. Before the conference, it was easy for the Vatican to uphold an unyielding position opposing artificial birth control. But sitting at a table in Egypt with men and women equally concerned about the future of humanity, Vatican officials seemed to realize that other issues were more important. Like them, we might wish that all moral positions could be settled ahead of time, but the reality of this, God's world design, is that the good is created, not applied; it results from collaboration, not isolated reflection; and it changes shape in different situations.

When we examine how moral precepts get started, we see that all our Lists of rights and wrongs are like this. The human race may be subject to divine morality, but that does not mean we define abstract categories such as "murder" and "lying" and say that everything in those categories is therefore "intrinsically" wrong. The absoluteness of morality means only that there is a difference between "truly" good and "only apparently good." It does not mean there has to be a set of actions that humans can classify under some concept like "cheating" or "adultery" and then mindlessly condemn every action listed under those headings. We have no warrant for restricting God's way of teaching to the deductive method. Indeed, on this planet, the best teachers more often use *in*duction: they patiently assist students in getting insights into their own experiences.

If God has preferred to educate humanity through the inner spirit responding to concrete situations, and writing laws to retain what has been learned, then what is truly good does not exist in a "general" vacuum. The human good is always the actual or the possible. Ideals such as honesty, loyalty, compassion, fairness, etc., are only conceptual pure types that we use as background for discerning right and wrong in the concrete. Experience tells us we cannot draw a straight line from fixed general concepts to fresh particular insights into concrete right and wrong anyway. For example, people agree that disloyalty is generally wrong, but will argue that *this* act of theirs was not really "disloyal." People agree that murder is wrong, but disagree whether abortion is always murder.

The good life, then, is ever insecure. We seldom say, with certitude, "This is right" or "This is wrong." There is usually a mental reservation going on: "If what I am told is true . . ." or "If this will really be the consequence, . . ." And we take a risk. Being good is a matter of pushing history forward a little from the present situation, inherited from imperfect people, to what we hope is a somewhat improved situation. We stand in hope—both because we are half-blind discerners of right and wrong and because the heirs to whom we hand on the situations are too.

Morality still has a direct connection to death, though one unlike a bank teller tallying accounts at the day's end. We still approach our deaths with a questionable résumé, not knowing for sure what good we have done. In some cases, we did good deeds sheerly for self-gain. In others, we acted altruistically but hurt someone anyway. Is there something wrong with being morally uncertain? I don't think so. In God's providence, it seems better to be unable to list the good we've done. If God has no List of things we shouldn't do, then neither should we keep our List of good things we did. And when we think of the people whose integrity we admire, don't we always see people who don't bother keeping moral records? Aren't they loath to boost their own grades and to mentally quiz others on their moral worth?

Again, having to live with moral uncertainties and to make mistakes out of that uncertainty can be quite discouraging without faith that God is somehow at work here. Many pious adults will blanch at this prospect and return to The List for assurance. For them, The List is God enough.

DOES GOD PUNISH?

"My belief in a God who punishes is firmly based on my experience of rush-hour traffic. Those weavers especially. If they don't pay somehow, I'll have words with God."

This sentiment is not as shallow as it sounds. Think of the horrors of terrorism and torture. Think of child molesters who are never caught. The world is not a just place. It never has been and never will be. So it is natural for those who believe in an afterlife to hope in a divine "getting even."

If you could go back in time to November 2, 1948 and observe any Catholic church in North America, you'd see the very curious manner in which this hope in divine justice was expressed. All day long, men and women, girls and boys, would emerge randomly one-by-one from every door of the church, turn around, and head back in. Five minutes later, out they'd come, around they'd turn, and in they'd go again. What they were doing was the once-a-year work of buying parole for the souls of the dead confined to Purgatory before they could move on to Heaven. Six Our Fathers, six Hail Marys, six Glory Be's, and out popped another soul. Boing.

Also, as the nuns instructed us, you could designate exactly which souls you wanted out. Unless someone beat me to it, I sprung my grandfather John, for example. And when you ran out of names, you could designate certain categories, such as "the soul who has longest sentence." That considerate thought, however, turned out to be more complicated than first appeared. Sister Grace Ellen was stumped when we pointed out a bias in the system. As long as lots of people were nominating the soul with the most years to go, it was to your advantage to die with a long string of venial sins, and hence a long sentence, particularly on November 2nd, say, mid-afternoon.

Besides, the souls who *really* had the longest sentence were hidden in the middle somewhere, stuck there simply because we, their survivors, had no formula for giving them anything like the priority we gave to "the last soul." The "middle" soul could be gotten out; the "100th soul" had a chance; the "soul who had fewest friends" had reason to be optimistic. But that left lots whose predicament could not be adequately described. OK, pray for "those whose predicament we cannot adequately describe" and . . . oh, well.

Even granting that this somehow benefited the dead, I cannot think of any benefits for the living, except that some of us developed a mindset that achieves respectable scores on computer games. Unfortunately, few church leaders saw the need to lead growing children to a more adult, more intelligible view of how God deals with sin and death. No doubt, these shepherds in the forties lived before modern psychology had worked out how our minds develop as we grow up. But even today, psychology has not sufficiently helped us deal with death. With our emotions, yes; but with our faith, no. With grieving, yes; but with hope, no. With anger, yes; but with commending our spirit into the hands of God, no.

Anyway, one very helpful insight into how to think about our own deaths lies not in modern psychology but in ancient psychology.

Aristotle noted that the mind can ask two very different kinds of questions—*what* and *whether*. The *what* question asks for a description or an explanation. About death we naturally ask *what* happens, *where* do we go, *how* it unfolds. Answers to these questions are long and metaphorical. That is, we can only give analogies about *what* happens.

However, the *whether* question asks for simple affirmations. Yes or no. About death we ask *whether* it is our total elimination or *whether* God somehow loses nothing worthwhile. We ask *whether* all shall be well and *whether* the entire universe has its fullest meaning beyond death. Answers to these questions are not metaphorical at all. We can say that death is not the end or that death is the end. We can say God created the universe, even though *what* happened at creation is much disputed. We can affirm that, yes, God gives us the wherewithal to make our lives meaningful, to overcome whatever is the enemy of our nature, and to face our deaths with an assurance that whatever good we did will remain in eternity. *What* will make our lives meaningful and *what* good we did remain hidden.

About Purgatory, all a Catholic can say is that, yes, God makes good out of evil. The sins we committed are somehow purged from us. *What* God might do to achieve this we cannot say, and yet we need some description, some palpable image, to support our belief. Parents try stifling evil in their children through rewards and punishment, and it is this system that children appropriately expect God to use. Hence, the reward of Heaven, the punishment of Purgatory and Hell. But fire and time are only metaphors for the reality.

Still, we need metaphors. So why not clothe our adult affirmations of faith with metaphors taken from the ways adults make good out of evil? Our metaphors for God's love should be based on how mature adults love, not on childhood or romantic varieties. Mature adults have learned that punishment and reward are only provisional supports to living a decent life. Eventually a person ought to pursue life along the paths of intelligence and reasonableness, responsibility and love. Mature, loving persons share burdens. They live in some measure of anxiety despite their reputation of being at peace. They put the commonweal above personal gain. All of this means some regular involvement in suffering. So, perhaps a better metaphor for the fate of evil in our lives lies in the suffering borne by those who love. In other words, if anyone suffers in some Purgatory, it is God. God's agony is the suffering of a lover eager to forget and itching to embrace the beloved. God's agony is the agony of any good person absorbing the worst that evil can do rather than perpetuate the evil to protect the self.

I am speaking metaphorically still. Our purgatorial suffering will perhaps be limited to seeing, with absolute clarity and in a single view, all the ways we slap God in the face and all the ways God welcomes us with love anyway. It is the purgative experience of having our faults overlooked and forgotten by someone deeply in love with us. It is purgative in the sense of a catharsis, a welcome elimination of useless baggage. Standing maskless before God, we burn, not from fire but from a poignant mixture of shame and gratitude.

We should not forget those sanctimonious frauds who prefer the sour justice of making amends, those who want to purchase Heaven by penance, those who are afraid of the embarrassing extravagance of God's ecstatic welcome. We can spot them in how they scold the imperfect. Come death, they're in for a quite an embarrassing, scathing purgation of divine forgiveness for their self-righteousness. At least we can hope so.

A FORGIVING GOD?

Somehow I find it difficult to think of Matty Ventresca worried whether or not God is forgiving. No doubt, Matty had his share of petty lies and meanness, but he grew up in a family that welcomed him despite both his peccadillos and his handicaps. They didn't forgive him anything before opening their doors. They took him as he was and delighted in his company. Their hospitality is not just a metaphor for how God acts. For Matty, it was the ordinary, day-to-day revelation of how God acts. Any religious sentiments he carried were massively influenced by how his adoptive parents cared for him. The idea of God having to forgive was probably far from his mind.

Most religions teach that God is infinitely forgiving. That made sense to me when I was young, but not so much because I ever thought God might abandon me. For me, forgiveness was about scrubbing out small black smudges on my soul. I believed God wanted me clean, though I had no doubt I'd be accepted lovingly were I to arrive dirty. With adults, however, for whom distinguishing right from wrong depends ultimately on conscience and intelligence rather than on authorities and laws, this moral fly-specking is the work of an Accountant God. This is a God who's pretty mad about our breaking the rules but who condescends to forgive anyway because of how bad we feel.

We have discussed the possibility that there really is no eternal list of rights and wrongs. If this is the case, if what is good is what results from intelligent and responsible choice, then God is simply not interested in passing any sort of after-the-fact judgment. God is far more preoccupied with helping people win their lives. If there is any passing of judgment on us, we do it to ourselves.

This is clear in an often-overlooked chapter in the Adam and Eve story that describes what happened to Cain after he killed Abel. God did not impose a capital punishment on Cain. With profound irony, Cain judged himself. His deepest fear was that he might be murdered. He ended up begging God to protect him from people who kill—people like himself. So God put a mark on his forehead, with the warning that whoever killed Cain would inherit a sevenfold vengeance.

This is an irony that marks everyone's conscience. Our deepest fears are that people like ourselves will cross our path. Just as the murderer Cain feared murderers, so thieves fear robbers, slanderers fear rumor-mongers, charlatans fear fakes, seducers fear seduction, and so on. God has no need to condemn our wrongdoing; we condemn ourselves. Any final judgment by God will be unlike the sentencing of a courtroom judge. It will be more like God's final decision to honor what we have chosen. With resignation, God will finally give up inviting the fearful to give up fearing. Unable to reverse the effects of our free choices, God will have failed to turn the hearts of those who covet the neighbor's goods or spouse.

That the Last Judgment is essentially a self-judgment is clear in what I believe is the most terrifying story in the New Testament—The Prodigal Son. Briefly, a father has two sons. The younger has the itch to get away and the elder more obediently stays home. The younger asks the father for his inheritance, which he gets, and then heads out, wasting it all on wine, women, and song. He eventually returns home, head hung in shame, hoping for a modest place among his father's servants. The father, who all this time has longed for his son's return, welcomes him with warm embrace, robe, ring, and celebration. Meanwhile, the elder brother complains that he has been faithfully laboring in the fields all these years, and where is the celebration for him?

There Jesus' parable ends. It may more aptly be called The Irked Brother, since Jesus aimed the parable directly at the Pharisees, who were claiming lifelong adherence to the rules and were irked because Jesus paid attention to their less holy fellows in religion. Like the Pharisees, the older brother in the story resented that the father would welcome home a foolish son.

Notice that the father never exactly forgives the prodigal; forgiveness is just not on his mind. He mainly is overjoyed that the son wants to be with him, and so he wants to celebrate. To the upright brother (that's you, Pharisee!) he gives the same invitation to join the celebration: "The doors of heaven are wide open. Come and celebrate with God—and all those God welcomes. There are no locks in the afterlife.

Come into Heaven whenever you please . . . unless, of course, you don't like the company."

Jesus had the insight that what makes separation from God a harrowing torment is that the damned repeatedly choose it for themselves. No one else damns them. Hell is identical to the refusal to accept the free gift of company with God. The Pharisees, Jesus implies, run an extreme risk of losing taste for a God who enjoys sharing a good time. Should they do so, then the free choice of damnation is theirs alone. Jesus skillfully ends the story without telling the Pharisees (or us) whether the brother lets go of his bitter righteousness. Thus, the obedient are easily damned. Terrifying, yes?

So, if God doesn't even bother much with forgiveness, if Jesus' picture of the father in this story is an accurate picture of God, then it really does not make much difference how certain we should be about our moral standing. What really does count, maybe the only thing that counts, is that we desire to be with our kind God and with the other fumbling mortals with whom we share the universe—along with everything else Jesus made a special point to mention: the veal entrée, the classy outfits, the finest jewelry, the music, the hugs, the dancing, and all our friends.

Somehow I can better picture Matty at this party than with a God who keeps records.

THE GOD WE FIND IN DEATH

We have looked more closely at death in order to understand more about God and about the kind of faith we need to meet death. With this approach, we have already presumed something that takes faith to believe, namely, that death is God's idea for sharing divine life with us. That belief alone has the power of leading us to a profound and yet practical trust that God would not allow death to be the end of us. Not that this trust is easy. Anyone who cares for the dying with this is mind will still find it difficult to accept the pain a dying person usually goes through. The friends and family of a person facing a terminal illness typically go through the same stages of dying—denial, anger, depression, bargaining, and, after some shuttling among these responses, acceptance. However, there is a profound difference between an acceptance that is just resignation and an acceptance that is full of hope. When a loved one dies, almost everyone eventually accepts the fact, but to carry on with mere resignation is nothing like carrying on with confidence that all shall be well.

To help support this difficult act of faith, we needed to reconsider seven common images of God. We needed to strip each image of various misleading impressions they often convey. But notice that it was not enough to replace these images by some alternative images. We also needed to state propositions—declarative sentences that call for an assent of the mind, not a picture in the imagination. It is these declarative sentences that point to the realities we believe in. Here, for example, are some of the major statements we offered for this assent:

> Hope is a real event, experienced by everyone, an event regarded everywhere as a key to something bigger than death.
>
> If there is any universal pattern in the universe that science reveals, it is clear that destiny everywhere involves a kind of death, not a death by annihilation but a death by an incorporation.
>
> It remains extremely important to use the mind simply to acknowledge and reverence the ultimate mystery of the universe and its divine origins and destiny.
>
> Despite the common belief that God saves individuals while communities become irrelevant, there is no individual immortality without a communal immortality.
>
> Deep in God's character, there may be a kind of frailty that has eternal worth.
>
> God wants to build life *with* us on earth, not just *for* us on some land beyond.
>
> God has preferred to educate humanity through the inner spirit responding to concrete situations, and inspires some to write laws only to retain what has been learned.
>
> Our metaphors for God's love should be based on how mature adults love, not on childhood or romantic varieties.
>
> If God doesn't bother much with forgiveness, then it really does not make much difference how certain we should be about our moral standing.
>
> The "Last Judgment" is essentially a self-judgment.

These are only some of the many propositions that follow from the basic belief that death belongs to God's way of sharing life with us—the divine life that remains ever mysterious, remote to our understanding yet intimate to our desires. At any one of the many deaths any person goes through, God is revealed. To meet these deaths with faith means accepting death as the price of life and, as well, learning intimate truths about God.

CHAPTER 4
The Law of Care

Science and the poet are one in matters mortal:
Death is not a random killer, reckless.
An end in every moment, the spine of evolution,
It strings our pearls to make a lovely necklace.

Our reflections have been largely negative. We debunked myths, looked at beliefs that contradict Judeo-Christian teachings, and criticized some mainline Judeo-Christian beliefs. Maybe we have disturbed even some of the beliefs that sustain the Ventresca family. And yet, whatever their beliefs, their *actions* suggest that their attitudes toward God and death braced them to meet life's agonizing challenges. What secret might they possess? How is it that despite the influence of misleading myths about death they would adopt a child with a terrible life-shortening illness and call him their own? What do they know that helps them live unflinchingly with death? And can we learn from them?

I think the answer is Yes. What they know is very simple: *Caring is more important than anything*. In the face of great odds, and going against any logical analysis of costs and benefits, they adopted Matty and raised him. Caring, for them, was more important than personal comfort. More important than an unruffled family life. And for whatever reason Matty's natural parents gave him up for adoption, the Ventresca's sense of care redeemed an awful situation.

This idea that caring is more important than anything is entirely consistent with modern views on the cosmos, the psyche, human history, and evolution. More than consistent, I would like to suggest that the idea of caring can make sense of a great many insights coming from astronomy, psychology, and the study of history. Briefly, here is the idea: There is a law at work in the universe—the law we referred to in Chapter 3. Under this law, there is a process at work by which love tends to emerge in the long run. It does not emerge automatically, the way trees grow from seeds, but the manner in which it does emerge is intelligible. This law is verifiable from empirical evidence yet it has been recognized by only a few philosophers and theologians. It has been called by various names, but for the sake of our discussion, let us call it "The Law of Care."

THE EVIDENCE FOR THE LAW

Recall what happened to your heart when you read the story of Matty Ventresca. You cared, did you not? There were events that occurred in your heart and mind, events that connected you to this little boy now dead. Now think of these events in the very large context of the universe of the astronomers. What happened in you was always possible, from the Big Bang on. In other words, matter has always had the potential of spirit within it, and upon your reading of Matty's story that spiritual event took place in you.

Caring happens all the time and everywhere. One day, while walking through a woods, I saw the corpse of a little starling hanging by one leg from the crotch of a sapling, and, while other birds chirped on and squirrels gamboled about, I suddenly broke down in tears. I am no fan of starlings, so I had to wonder what strange compassion erupted there.

It seems as though we are laden with care about the life of things. Some care is a joy, like the Hallmark-card-care for a beautiful baby. But most care really is a burden, a kind of weight on our hearts. It interrupts our otherwise smooth-running lives. It takes effort to ignore beggars on the street. We resent the hovering presence of the needy around us. We tell ourselves we have to reserve our energies for those for whom we are responsible: our children, spouse, friends, and relatives. But the argument is thin; it neither justifies ignoring those outside our social circles nor silences the grunts of care within us as news of people in need reaches our ears.

Although these cares seem to us like intrusions from the outside, they are just as much intrusions from within. It is our heart that intrudes, not just sound waves. St. Augustine described his caring as something ponderous. "My love is a weight," he said. Care has an inertia resembling that of a great ship: it is difficult to get one moving but, once in motion, it is just as difficult to stop.

Caring not only feels heavy, it also moves without our permission. It can waft us to the skies as we fall in love. It can pitch us down an emotional well as we reach out to others in need. Although care's inertia resists changing direction, we often manage to divert its natural movement into some tightly controlled response. Sometimes we stifle it altogether, but that requires work. The heart, being naturally warm, requires insulation from the movements of care if it is going to stay cold.

Everyone in the world is like this: caring. Certainly, much caring is misplaced; some of it is completely suppressed. But the best of social institutions result not just from human intelligence. It is not creativity alone that makes for a civilization. When life together works, it is a result from humans caring about humans. There is a very real network of love at work among people on our planet. It is as real as an apple we bite into. It may not be visible or audible; we can't touch it or taste it. But everyone experiences it.

Just because anyone's direct experience of caring can't be measured with yardsticks or meters, this is no reason why we cannot understand this experience as data on hard reality. There are invisible but very real things going on all the time. We are swamped by realities that we can never touch or taste. Let me give a mundane example. One day, standing at the top of our basement stairs, I accidentally nudged my tennis shoe over the edge of the step. Like a tiger released from its cage, it leapt down two steps, then four, and then, in a final great bound, banged onto the basement floor. I imagine that if the floor were not there to intercept it, my shoe would have kept on tumbling, headed for the center of the earth. It seemed as though some invisible beast had possessed my shoe and was lying in wait for the crucial nudge that would release it, leaping away full of motion and intention. Physicists, of course, avoid this kind of personification: a shoe has no plans, it doesn't "want" anything. They soberly proclaim a Law of Gravity, which predicts what my shoes and everything else physical will do when nudged over an edge. My point is that this Law of Gravity points to something quite real, yet invisible, inaudible, impalpable. It is not hiding in the shoe like a tiger. It cannot be located anywhere yet it works everywhere.

Why can this not be true for caring? It acts like a field of affective gravity permeating the universe. Like gravity, it follows laws. Caring has a consistent character and clear effects. Our minds may hesitate to accept a reality that cannot be pictured, felt, heard, touched, smelled or tasted, but, as we talked about earlier, matter is not everything. From the most rigid scientific point of view, adhering strictly to the scientific rule that reality is verified in evidence, a Law of Care seems to be what is going on. There are data all around us that point to some dynamic process in the universe, a process that blossomed when consciousness evolved. If this is true, then we reach a scientific conclusion that could set the course for scientists for the 21st century: Besides entropy dragging the physical substrata of the universe to a cold end, a Law of Care is working at higher strata and in the opposite direction.

Notice that we humans are not the only occurrences of caring. When a cat owner dies, a cat can become depressed. The fabled Lassie rescue stories have some basis in people's experience. We know dogs that act like pals to each other. Even at the plant level, we find that plants thrive when planted together, to say nothing of the evidence of plants thriving when spoken to. There's a pattern here whose substructure can be detected at the chemical and even atomic levels. If evolution has had this potential from the beginning, then the Milky Way was predisposed for this, headed toward caring. We, little specks floating in the Milky Way's great cloud, are its way of coming to care.

Earlier we compared this to the more familiar law, "Survival of the Fittest." According to this law, those species more equipped to survive will survive. The vagaries of chance allot poor odds to the vulnerable and the timid and they eventually vanish. This makes sense, up to a point. Survival of the Fittest is a model of elegance and simplicity that explains how higher forms survive and lower forms do not. But it relies on variations in genetic coding that are completely random, totally subject to chance. Think about it, though. Almost every random variation is a disaster. Mere chance has no bias toward more intelligible functioning. Without some other organizing force at work, even the one-in-a-million variation that promises to lift an organism to a higher plane must be capable of resisting the million variations that drag the organism down. But here we are, not only the supreme evidence that reality is headed somewhere, but surrounded by fantastically varied modes of adaptation and accommodation developed by living creatures everywhere. The eye of a minnow. The enterprise of a beaver. The sheer cleverness and complexity of higher forms suggest that, besides chance, matter contains another law, a law biased for higher organization based on spiritual activities.

Gradually, patiently, casually, the material universe played with its molecules and elements until cells replicated. Cells convened to form plants. Plants experimented with alternatives until consciousness and mobility emerged. Animals swam, crawled, and flew, expanding their range of conscious experience until some of them experienced the grasp of understanding, an insight. If the development of children mirrors the development of our species, this first insight probably occurred immediately before the first smile. Perhaps some hungry ape mistook a rock for an apple, and another ape grinned. From there, this slow but sure law unfolded the mind, created language, mastered the arts of hunting and agriculture, and developed civilization.

Again, matter is not everything. Whoever said it had to be? A child, perhaps, but not after growing up and recognizing the reality of such ordinary spiritual things as appreciation, insights, acknowledgment, promises, and praise. If matter is not everything, and we easily believe that matter is governed by laws of gravity and electromagnetism, then we should have no trouble believing there may be laws that govern events of consciousness.

We don't have to picture little cells "wanting" to be plants. Prehistoric primates aren't "trying" to be intelligent. Whatever dynamic it may be that leans matter toward spirit, it does not have to be carried consciously by its subjects. Hegel suggested there is a "Cunning of Reason" whereby history pursues its purposes totally indifferent to the intentions of individuals, as if History dangled a carrot in front of an asinine humanity for us to pursue, all the while dragging History's cart forward. But History does not have to be some super-subject, conscious of its own aims. It is enough to say that matter isn't everything and that it is biased toward spirit, whose future is unknown to us.

Whatever this higher law may be called, its most profound accomplishment is human caring. Caretaking is one of the highest achievements of our galaxy. The Law of Care dictates that wherever insights and feelings occur in the universe, there will also occur a movement that responds to any perceived needs. The universe has been headed toward the phenomena of care, and is now expanding its range as it assists us in our development of our social structures and our cultural values.

One of the fascinating features of the Law of Care is that it helps drive the evolution of our species in a double manner. We care about one another's welfare and about what we will become during our allotted span of years. That is, whenever we express care for others, we become more caring persons. We are changed together.

We may well wonder what kind of future our universe reserves for generations thousands of years from now who, we may hope, will have taken the Law of Care as seriously as our generation has taken the Law of Gravity.

A COMMUNITY-MAKING LAW

The Law of Care is not merely a network of exchange between people. It is not only a give-and-take between two parties. It is also a kind of glue that makes two parties one. More than *mutuality*, where we exchange with one another and give up what we have, care works through a *commonality*, where we give without losing and receive without taking. It is the mystery whereby humans can be part of one another without losing their individuality.

We notice what a large part of ourselves others have been when death has cut them off. We feel a huge gap. Like a tongue investigating the tooth recently abandoned by a filling, the heart keeps looking for the person that should be there. The ache throbs in every cell. Between every two thoughts, like a far-off echoing dirge, we sense a wailing grief. Not a cry one can hear. Rather a silence where there once was music. Something is missing, something vital, some part of ourselves.

How can one person be "a part of" another? If you are a vital part of me, and you die, has a vital part of me died? What exact part of me is gone? Most of us would answer that you miss what you love. A man you cared for is now gone. You grew accustomed to paying attention to him. And now, every time you feel the urge to say something, he's not there anymore. But this experience, true and poignant as it is, does not explain why we say, "a part of *me* is gone." You are not me, and I am not you. Yet I feel that something of me will die if you die, and vice versa.

It is not pure speculation that asks, What part of me is gone? Part of me *feels* gone. When friends die, something in *us* dies, and we wonder how I will live without them, what to let go and what to cling to. We ask it because in every meaningful relationship each party takes care to give and yet retain. But what to give and what to retain? In highly enmeshed relationships, the parties have given up too much of themselves, so that there is little autonomous self left. In more disengaged relationships, we dole out only carefully measured parts of ourselves, so that there is not much genuine commonality achieved. In every relationship, we daily make choices that aim to strike a balance between giving too much and giving too little. Perhaps, in a twisted effort to love you, I have let you make my decisions and suppressed my own best self. We often see this overdependence in immature relationships between spouses. But whatever balance has been struck, no matter how enmeshed or disengaged the relationship, when one partner dies, something has been killed in the survivor. Part of me—whether borrowed from my friend or unique to me—has died. The finest people we know talk like this. In fact, the rule seems to be that the finer the person, the *more* likely will we hear something like, "She was a part of me."

The way one person can be truly a part of another lies in a common but peculiar feature of human awareness. Awareness is always double, which becomes evident when we think about what it means to be "present." We can be "present" to the things around us as we notice them and think about them. A table at breakfast. A breeze blowing through our hair. But as we notice these things, we simultaneously are "present" to ourselves. That is, we are also aware of ourselves as noticers and thinkers. Let me give an example.

I am in the basement, gluing the pieces of a broken casserole lid. My mind is fixed on the glue, the clamp, and the pieces of glass. But I am also doing this as a conscious person, meaning I am present to myself as I do it. If a robot were doing it, it may perform the same actions, but the robot is not conscious. We might think of the robot as "aware" of the task because it takes in data, but it is not "aware" of itself. I, however, am aware of myself as a fixer of a lid at the same time that my attention is completely dedicated to the lid.

All human activity is like this. We have two very distinct ways of being aware, and they always go together. We are *attentive to objects* and we are *conscious of ourselves*. We attend to the matter at hand, and we are simultaneously conscious of ourselves paying attention. My sense of myself while working on a lid is not a general or abstract sense; it is a concrete sense of myself as a fixer-of-a-broken-lid. It is a sense of myself that changes. I have one very specific sense of myself when I'm wondering how to clamp odd-shaped pieces for gluing, and quite a different sense when I find a solution. But although we experience ourselves in different manners, this consciousness always accompanies human acts.

Once we look closely at how human acts are *conscious* acts—self-present acts—we will see that our acts make us aware not only of our *individual* selves as acting. They also make us aware of anyone acting along with us. When my wife and I cook, we pay attention to the stove, the spoon, the garlic; but we are conscious not only of ourselves as individuals but as ourselves as cooking together. If the phone rings and a friend asks, "What are you doing?", I don't say, *"I'm* cooking," I say, *"We're* cooking."

The same goes for nearly everything we do. Even if I'm at work alone, writing a report, I am also earning a salary for "us." It is we who are maintaining a life together here. Again, if someone asks, "What plans do *you* have for the weekend?", I respond, *"We* are going to my sister's." When you talk to me, you are talking to the "us" I am acting together with.

If my wife were to die, then I would feel the sting of her death in my consciousness—that is, in my very awareness of myself that accompanies almost every act of paying attention to anything. It is not the same agents paying attention anymore. It is just me, where it used to be us. And while I would miss her with all my heart, I would as much miss the "us" that we were.

Here we come to a question whose answer lies in the realm of faith. The question is deeply philosophical and yet, like all the good philosophical questions, one that practically everybody faces when a beloved dies, whether or not they believe in God. The question is this: When my friend has died, is it still "we" who carry on? Or am I left completely alone? I may pretend you are here by my side. I may imagine you up in heaven watching, smiling, telling God to take care of me. But am I just imagining things? Or is it true that the "we" who worked and played together while you were on earth is not dead? Am I being reasonable if I still talk to you?

If we answer Yes, if we acknowledge there is still something to the "we" that we were, then we can experience first-hand a remarkable phenomenon about the entire human race. That is, if "we" are not irrevocably fragmented at death, if there is at least some real meaning to "we" after a friend's death, then we cannot limit the circumference of ourselves merely to our circle of dear friends. What makes the human race a single entity is not just the great tree of biological ancestry. The solidarity of our race also shows in our experience of feeling like we are a part of one another. There have been thousands of people with whom each of us has collaborated during our lifetimes. They too form of a part of the "we" that each of us was conscious of when we worked together. This "we" interlocks over the entire globe, forming a single thing, one solidary reality that is the subject of human history.

This reality, this human family, lives on even though its members die. It is as real an object as one's own body. Although it cannot be seen, felt, tasted, or heard, there is an objective reality going forward in history. Memories may fade, but "we" continue through shared meaning. My dead parents live on in me, not only in the sense that I look and talk like them, not only because I am their biological offspring, and not only because I sometimes remind others of my parents. They live on as *part* of me to the extent I continue doing the things I used to do with them, the way they used to do them.

Not everything I did with my parents ought to live on, of course. They were not perfect. So it is left to me to purge from my life the less authentic habits I inherited from them. In doing this, I help redeem their lives. I filter out the ideas that wouldn't work; I reprioritize some of their values. I'm not perfect either. Those friends, colleagues, and relatives who survive me will have to do the same with my life as it intertwined with theirs. So I will forever be part of the Ventrescas, even though I never met Matty.

Once we see how people can really be parts of each other, we can understand what it means to share in the life we call "divine." Recall what we said in an earlier chapter, that God *creates* each of us with community and history in mind. To that insight, we can now add that God also *redeems* us through community and history. How so? To each of us is bequeathed a cultural sediment of both sense and nonsense as we enter the world. We try to spend our lives adding to the sense and subtracting from the nonsense. If it is true that the entire human family shares a common consciousness, then the entirety of God's work redeeming the human race is also *our* work. Redemption is not some legal status into which we fall without noticing. It is not some entity created by God that humans can never experience. It is not a pass/fail slip issued by a divine record-keeper. No, redemption is about *human collaboration* with God in putting meaning and value into life. It may be true that God alone redeems; but God does not redeem alone. God requires our cooperation, not only during our lives together but even after one of us is gone, as survivors carry on the ideals, roles, habits, preferences, insights, and commitments we achieved with the deceased and let go of our shared biases and foolishness.

If the divine—God—collaborates with the human, and if this divine is self-present in a manner similar to the consciousness of humans, then we can say quite precisely how we can be a part of God and God a part of us. I want to avoid here a picture of God "inside" each person, or vice versa. I'm after the more poignant understanding that our human acts are intrinsically collaborative with the divine. We are a part of God because our acts of intelligence and caring are collaborative acts with

God; we cannot understand and love relying on resources that are completely ours. This is a marvelous truth: The self to which I am present in all my conscious acts is not a solitary self. It is a shared self. The self to which I am present is also the divine other. The "internal me" inaccessible to others without my consent is a myth. There is no solitaire in a universe where God is the dealer. We play this game of life and death together.

So you, the Ventrescas, and I are a part of God if, as I believe, our reflecting together is God's own work.

WORKING WITH THE LAW

How might we take the Law of Care seriously? What practical steps can we take to embody it in our lives so that the law works in us more readily? We can look at the ways we say "goodbye."

Alice came to the hospital to pay her last visit to her old friend Jack. Jack's cancer was everywhere, and he and his wife had decided enough was enough. They pulled out the chemo drip and the feeding tubes. It would be just a matter of days.

So Alice held Jack's hand and told him she would pray for him. She told him she loved him. And as she was about to leave, she gave him a last hug and said, "Take care."

She felt stupid having said that. How can Jack "take care" anymore? Of course, she wanted to say "Good bye," but just couldn't bring herself to it. "Good bye" means "We'll never meet again."

Why is our departure language so awkward! It has not always been so. "Good bye" was once "God be with ye." It was our way of wishing someone good company on a journey. The emphasis was on what we wanted for someone else, not on what was going be lost to ourselves, which seems to be a prevailing mood in our culture. Perhaps we're awkward because we're self-centered. We may have lost the art of imagining ourselves in the other person's position, with another's hopes and fears, assurances and risks. We lack the easy ability to see both the dying person and ourselves, the survivors, as involved in an ordinary process of life. After all, dying is not only an experience for the dying person. The friends, relatives, and providers of care experience deep company with dying and are changed in the process as well.

Dying is something normal, something we hope our children will not ruin their lives trying to avoid. But because our particular culture has deemed death as the worst thing that could happen, death is excluded from life, death is life's appointed enemy. So the dying process becomes alien to life rather than a stage of living. We are oblivious to the fact that to be dying is to be living. So we don't know what to say to the dying.

Even "farewell," which, on its face, is a hopeful remark—I hope you fare well!—now carries the connotation of final closure. Like "Good bye," it practically means "This is final; this is death." So, to convey the fact that a parting is not final, we usually say, "See you later."

Now we have a new departure formula. "Take care of yourself." Or just "Take care." Before long we'll probably just say "'Care!" as we jump into the car and roar off. Maybe someday "'Care!" will slip down the same emotional slope and land with "Good bye" and "Farewell" and mean "This is final; this is death." But for now, it seems appropriate in most departures except the final one.

We genuinely hope people we love take care of themselves. Usually we feel that our friends should take *better* care of themselves than they are doing now. We're irked at their habits of self-punishment and their risky behavior. We feel convinced that, if it were possible, we would take better care of them than they do. Why is this? Why do we so easily presume that if our friends would allow us, we would protect them better, nourish them better, and guide their lives better than they do for themselves?

You might say we love them better than they love themselves. From our point of view, we feel waves of benevolence toward them with full confidence that they feel no such thing toward themselves. For their part, they say, "Oh, if you knew the real me, you wouldn't love me. You wouldn't even like me." Or, if they don't say it, they think it. They feel it.

This is odd. Usually we are quite confident that our love for others springs from a genuine and real perception of value in them. Yet when we are on the receiving end of that love, we have no confidence at all. "Your love for me is misplaced," we say. How is it I believe I can love you better than you love yourself but not believe you can love me better than I love myself? It hinges on a conviction deeply held by everyone—the conviction that we know ourselves better than anyone else does. We feel that others have no idea of the stupid ideas we've clung to in the past. We are sure that no one has any idea of the sometimes malicious feelings in our hearts. We're convinced if some of our secret deeds and practically all our thoughts were known, our would-be friends would withdraw in horror.

This conviction, however, is only half true. The true half is that, yes, we know more *facts* about ourselves than anyone else can. The untrue half is the conclusion that therefore we must know better what is *valuable* about ourselves than anyone else can. But is this conclusion valid? Since when are we the most objective judges of our worth? Our experience should remind us that we often take pride in our silly parts and we are too timid about our precious parts. Our close friends often disagree with us about our best and worst qualities. Our look at this from their side: We look on those we love and feel a deep conviction of their worth. We believe that our appreciation of them is far deeper than they will ever have by themselves.

We must consider the possibility that this strange imbalance on self-assessment may be how divine wisdom set it up. God may well have designed things so that we need each other to understand our worth. To the degree that this is the case, it follows that self-made individualists must really be clueless about their own worth. This is because only those who love us have the best view of what is good and bad in us. We should know this from our childhood. It is the eye of love in our parents that sees what is best in us and what we should get rid of. It is the eye of love in our friends that knows what we are capable of, and where we may have bought bigger boots than we could ever fill. I don't know anyone who can accurately assess his or her worth alone. Being cared for is our best hope for becoming what our Creator, in collaboration with nature and our friends, wants us to be.

Sometimes, when we are about to leave town, we tell someone to take care of himself or herself while we're gone. This is a fine sentiment, but very difficult to take seriously when you're on the receiving end. Once, I had visited my sister Kathleen and her family for a few days, and, as I was getting into the car to leave, she said, "You buckle up now! We want you alive!" This was some years ago, before buckling up was either my personal habit or state law. But reluctantly I buckled up and, during the ensuing hours, could feel her caring pressure across my chest. Here I was, taking care of myself because she wanted me to. It felt strange, but it also felt deeply right.

We usually don't think of ourselves as precious cargo, especially when driving. But that is what each one of us is. When our families or friends tell us to be "careful," this seems to be God's way of telling us we are lovable. We learn it through people who hug us, who snap our seat belts in place, who say to us "You take care now," And whose look adds, " . . . or else!"

The moral of this story seems to be, Get Pushy with Those You Love. Help them feel the pressure of your love. It is not enough to just stand ready, waiting for them to ask for help. Standing by doesn't tell them they are worth unfathomable care; it tells them only that you like keeping your distance. The normal way God's love really reaches people is through people getting aggressive with their care. In this, God works through the Law of Care.

It is up to us, then, to cooperate with the Law of Care. Indeed, this law cannot work at the human level without occurrences of decisions to care. The more we do this to one another while we live, the easier it will be for all of us to face death. The more we realize our worth in the eyes of others, the easier it is to believe that our death is not the end, that our worth has an eternal, deathless core. At the same time, it is easier for the survivors if they know the dying person is being carried to the mysterious beyond supported by their love.

Perhaps if Alice had been more pushy with her care for Jack while he was healthy, chances are an exchange of glances would have been enough at the end—glances that said, "We have walked together. And, to the limits which mystery allows, we always shall walk together."

HOW CARE MAKES COMMUNITY IMMORTAL

Together with God. One with the divine. One with the universe. These phrases suggest visions experienced only by Buddhist monks. Truth is, they are not visions; they are realities. Nor are they uncommon; they are quite ordinary. Simply because we are humans living in community we share in the divine life.

But what is it about "community" that is so divine? Sartre thought that other people were Hell itself. Reinhold Niebuhr proposed that while individuals can be moral, communities are necessarily immoral. Even cloistered nuns can drive each other nuts. Yet we admire the Ventrescas for the life they shared with Matty. But why do we find this admirable? What values are present there? Can we put in words how godly these humans seem to us?

We suggested earlier that the presence of hope in human hearts points to a kind of immortality—one that can be found in the deathless character of human community. Now that we have seen how the Law of Care permeates the universe, and in particular how each person can be a part of another, we can make clear just how we, by being members of community, beat death and share in divine life.

Earlier we reflected on how the presence of death forces us to take responsibility for our individual lives. However, in claiming that responsibility, we always find ourselves including others as the object of our concern and care. And the manner in which we watch out for others makes us immensely more distinguishable among our fellows than animals are among theirs. True, humans *look* different from one another in ways animals do not, but we *act* differently to each other person because our engagements and promises are so unique.

So our individuality is always achieved through a give-and-take with our communities. Part of our self-making means finding the appropriate balance between taking responsibility for our personal beliefs and taking on the beliefs of our community. Although for centuries thinkers have flopped the balance back and forth between the primacy of the isolated individual and the primacy of the community with its organically-linked members, we should not dismiss the significance of the community in the meaning of our individual lives.

To see the transcendent dimension of community in our lives, it is important to let go of the notion that we are just a collection of individuals. Despite the crucial importance of individual responsibility in making each of us unique, the notion that we carry the meaning of our lives completely with ourselves as individuals makes little sense. Almost every value we cherish, and viewpoint we take, we received from others. And we continue to carry them with others so that as these values and meanings shift and evolve, they do so throughout the entire group.

To cast this same thought in the symbolic terms of the Hebrew and Islamic scriptures, we can say that God's idea of Adam and Eve was not a blueprint for an individual. It was preëminently a blueprint for community. We make blueprints the same way. When we design something, we start with the whole picture and work out the parts in light of the whole. An engineer, for example, does not start designing a lawnmower by sketching a cotter pin. It seems reasonable to assume that when God conceived the idea of humanity, it was essentially an idea of community; the design of individuals took shape from there; it made no sense outside of community.

To use another symbol, we can say that God did not create us like a gardener plants tulips. You and I are not individual bulbs God buried in earth and will pluck when we die. God did not want a mere assortment of flowers. God wanted to create a living web, a family of people. God wanted us to be interconnected, bringing new meanings to the world together.

The Genesis statement that we are created in God's image and likeness is an observation about the entire human family, not about each member. God did not fashion *individuals* in the divine image and likeness, one after another like a cookie cutter. God fashioned an entire people destined to live in community over time. The implication here is that if we want to see the best image of God in humanity, we will not find it in any one person. We will find it best in a loving community. A Mother Teresa, by herself, does not reveal the full depths of God. It is Mother Teresa *with* her sisters, *with* the dying, sharing what life they have at the moment. We find God not exactly *in* each other but, more precisely, *between* each other. We find God in *events* among individuals, not in monadic individuals conceived as a walking pack of virtues.

The statuary in the high Christian churches gives the opposite message: the saints represented in stone are almost exclusively alone, as if their entire significance were as a model of individual virtue, with an independent line to God. Shouldn't our sculptors look with a theological eye at what made saints really saintly? For example, take the four famous saints of the Renaissance: Ignatius Loyola, Martin Luther, John of the Cross, and Teresa of Avila. Christian imagination usually enshrines them on an altar labeled "mystics" because they experienced intense exaltations in prayer and an indescribable sense of intimacy with God. Yet it is not for their individual mysticism that we should honor them. They were essentially *reformers*. They consciously set out to shape a community responsive to God and responsive to humanity. While they loved God with all their hearts, they were consumed with a passion to create a community of people who made a difference. This is the way the love of God works. We don't exactly pour out our love for God. We *receive* God's love flooding our hearts, which is a love for the world, the neighbor, the community.

Like most good art, the reason the statues were first carved is not always the reason they have subsequently been kept. Their disciples commissioned sculptures in order to authorize them in a church top-heavy with stubborn ecclesiastics. By depicting in stone their intimate relationship with God, artists conferred a popular ordination upon them which lent legitimacy to their reformations. Naturally, these reformers also stood as examples of individual virtue—a notion prized in the 1500s as much as social awareness is today. Unfortunately, once church heavyweights finally acknowledged that these reformers deserved a hearing, these artworks served in later centuries mainly to make a religious ideal out of individual mystical experience rather than communal reform. But the facts remain: mystics they certainly were; but the major effects of their private, mystical experiences upon others were in the area of social structures, discipline, education, law, and culture.

This brings us to a surprising conclusion: Solitary prayer seems *not* the ordinary place where we experience God. We *experience* God in our dealings with each other far more often than in monkish meditation. In meditation we may come to *understand* such ordinary experiences and perhaps to see God more clearly. And, true, occasionally we experience a great rush of love in prayer. However, the function of prayer is to help us bring to a good end the experience of God that comes from being involved with others. Here, in social intercourse, is where the image and likeness of God become visible, more so than within the confines of any individual, no matter how holy.

Despite the misleading statuary, in most religions we can find aspects of this communitarian view of God and of ourselves. Few, if any, religions speak of God exclusively as "a person." Ancient Greek and Egyptian myths saw the heavens as populated with mobs of gods. Some American aborigines, like many polytheistic cultures, associate different gods with the sun, the forest, the moon, the running waters, the caves, and many forces of nature. Shintoism probably holds the record with about 800,000 gods, each associated with a distinct place. In the Koran, even though "There is no other God but Allah," we can read,

> *We* made the sperm into a clot of congealed blood. Then of that clot *We* made a lump. Then *We* made out of that lump bones and clothed the bones with flesh. Then *We* developed out of it another creature. So blessed be God!

Similarly, the God of the Hebrew Bible said,

> Let *us* create the human in *our* own image and likeness.

It may well be that the "we" and "us" in these passages represent the authors' view that God works with a heavenly court, but it is still God in community that provides the blueprint for humanity. In the three centuries after Christ, Christians came to call God a "trinity" of persons. So the evidence is everywhere that we do not always think of God as alone, no more than we think of ourselves always as alone. Rather, the reason for our social nature is found in God's social nature.

We have been created like unstable atoms, eager to share electrons with other atoms in order to avoid a chaotic existence and to become part of something bigger than our solitary selves. When we reach out to one another, whether to give or to receive, we expect that the significance of human connections, no matter how brief, is somehow permanent.

With this understanding, we can look again at what our universal yearning for "immortality" involves. We needn't be mesmerized by unending life. We can look instead to love and community. Personal experience bears this out, telling us that love must be somehow at the heart of the immortal object of our hope. The ever-recurring movements of love in human hearts, even though we may not carry them out very well, put demands on the human spirit that are to be obeyed. The very fact that the human communities that last longest seem to be those that maintain a culture of love and mutual support makes for solid historical evidence that any positive meaning to be found in the death of an individual lies in love and community.

This love has immortality written all over it. It gives a stamina to carry on despite the threat of death. It prompts us to reach out to the neighbor and to build communities that will outlast us. Like the wind, it gusts without warning and is invisible in an even more total sense. It bursts out whenever we look on others and our hearts want to care. It can blossom even when our contact with others is quite remote. It happens when a computer analyst discovers demographic patterns of illness. It happens when a director of welfare must deal with managers, who must deal with supervisors, who must deal with social workers, who, finally, touch the hands of persons in need. This force can often care more effectively through the instrumentality of economic spreadsheets.

That is not all. In the first Letter of John, we read that God *is* love. (This is not an answer to the question, What is love?—Answer, *God* is love. Rather it is an answer to the question, What is God?—Answer, God is *love*.) The same belief can be found in most other theistic religions. If it is literally true that God is love, then human community is not merely "modeled after" divine community. To create us in the divine image means not only molding individuals who are shaped by their families and friends. It means more than the creation of the world, of Eve and Adam. It means that God is the very activity of mutual affection and care that binds us to one another. In this sense, God *continues* to create, constantly. God creates wherever we care for one another. In these engagements, where love comes alive, God comes alive. In these engagements we can see more than the image and likeness of God in the flesh. We see God; because God *is* the love we bear.

If this is how God creates, and if the human condition includes both a mortality and an immortality, at least we can see where immortality lies. The immortality we feel in our bones has already begun. It flashes out in mutuality. Divinity reveals itself in community. Our efforts to share with one another remain good eternally because the love that fills them is the living essence of an eternal God. Time will not destroy them.

So we can reconsider our fear of death. If we fear that death will separate us from our loved ones, isn't that fear really part of our desire to love well? If we fear death because it threatens to put an end to our loving, then that "fear" is not a fear of death itself but rather fear of love lost. Imagine a fifty-year-old man learning that he has a terminal illness. Typically, he will wish that God give him a few more years to carry out some business he considers unfinished. This is less a fear of death as a fear that his care for others may end prematurely. All these very human hopes to beat death are, in reality, part of a desire to enrich the family. What we spontaneously regarded as a fear of death is really a fear that our love will be frustrated. But if love is God, and so bears the immortality of irrevocable meaning, it follows that no love is lost. At a minimum, we ought to be grateful that God gives this love to us, even though we cannot control how many years we will have to make our love effective. At a maximum, we can be grateful that God works that love in us.

We can also be discerning about what is genuine love and what is a cheap imitation. We can easily confuse genuine neighborly love with more shameful hopes to enjoy the appreciation and awe of others. If our fifty-year-old man with the terminal illness worries more about his good name than about his good deeds, then he has reason to fear death. Death will snatch him up in the midst of his self-concern. The more we mistake fame and power for genuine love, the more reason we have to fear that our life has no genuine meaning and, consequently, the more reason to fear the day when death renders that fraudulent living irreversible. This is because the desire for fame and power corrupt the community, which is to say that they corrupt what is truly immortal. And when you corrupt what is truly immortal, you become very, very mortal.

Let us step back now and see what these reflections have to say about the Law of Care. We noted that while this law does not work in any automatic fashion, it works in an intelligible way nonetheless. It makes sense, but not the kind of sense that we discern by studying cause and effect, or studying statistical odds, or studying the predictable growth of a plant. Rather it is the kind of sense that we discern in the give-and-take of friendships. We cannot predict much about the future of a friendship, but as it unfolds, it makes sense anyway. And while we cannot ignore those friendships that break down, when they do, we can discern the reasons for the breakdown. While it takes insight into each stage of a friendship's growth or decline to understand that friendship, we cannot fully understand it without acknowledging the key role played by care in each party. Mutual care, and the enhanced care for others that overflows from strong friendships, together comprise the dynamic process behind every genuine growth. They likewise are the key element that degenerating friendships lack.

When that care does emerge, then the partial meanings of individuals find their full coherence and sense in the shared meanings of individuals who care for each other. Where individuals pull back and attempt to rely on their internal resources alone, we find less and less sense, smaller and smaller frameworks of coherence, and larger and larger fears. In the end, we find an awful mortality. Not only was a potential community annihilated, its potential members see in its failure just evidence that caring is not worth it. They look elsewhere for something to make sense out of life, confining their search to the immediate and the transient, hypersensitive to their fear of other people, and erecting psychic barriers to the workings of the Law of Care that urges psychic openness to others. The death that warrants genuine fear, then, is the death that results from suppressing our native penchants to grow in care for each other.

HOW CARE MAKES HISTORY IMMORTAL

The Law of Care is not without its dark side. No matter how deep our faith and readiness to meet death, the onset of death remains a threat of loss. Indeed, most of us carry aches in our hearts over loved ones who have died.

In particular, we have been recalling the story of Matty Ventresca, comparing his life to our own, and finding in him an Everyone who ever came to be, who lived and who dies. This remembering is good. Without it, we would have no forebears to rely on, only on ourselves and the wits of our peers. Without stories like Matty's we would be unsure whether a risk like adopting a handicapped baby was worthwhile. But we cannot help but feel that Matty's death was something bad, a tragedy, an unforgettable loss.

When I remember my dear departed, I think of it in terms of loss. I lost my friend Leo. I lost my friend Michael. I lost my friend Marion. I lost my friend Donna. I lost my mother, Nola. I lost my father, Walter. I lost my brother, Bob. I lost my wife's father, Otto, and her mother, Dorothy. I lost a wonderful colleague, Prudie. Like a *sotto voce* subtheme echoing under the lyrics, a cello hums a slow cadenza as I endure the deaths of those I love.

"Lost." What a silly way to say they died. They were never mine to lose. They were never a possession I could misplace. And I still play their memories over and over, as if by remembering I might assist their immortality.

But I have noticed lately that I've been oversimplifying them, reshaping them, telling myself lies (if truth be told) making memory more an emblem of their beauty and goodness rather than an accurate account of what really went on between us. I suppose I would not make a reliable biographer. So there we are: my remembering has really been for *my* sake; I wanted something simple and good to cherish. Inadvertently I have been making a possession out of them for my own peace of mind. "I lost them" is apropos after all.

I even "lost" some dear friends who are not dead. We parted at some fork in life's road and, after glimpsing each other through the trees now and then, became too divergent to see anything but the road ahead. A few years ago, I serendipitously bumped into such a friend at a K mart. It felt like an old dream coming true, until I looked again. My dream had betrayed me. The friend I knew was replaced with someone both toughened and weakened by life so much that I could not find the original thread that once tied us together. I somehow lost the words in my heart that used to come so naturally with her. Our paths remained diverged even when they crossed.

Such a waste, that a person—that living entity made wonderful through relationships—comes to an end. Even though you and I go on, the persons we were for each other can be lost.

When we lose someone, we lose far more than a companion. Eventually we also lose all memory of the departed. Were I to die tomorrow, the funeral parlor might bustle with people telling stories about me. But were I to die thirty years from tomorrow, a few hobbling old acquaintances would be dropped off by younger relatives. They might agreeably disagree about how old I was and what year it was that I did such-and-such. Mostly, they won't remember much.

So even the stories die. I look at old photos of my grandparents, regretting that I didn't ask more questions when I was young. Now, no one can tell me anything about them except the bare skeletons of their stories formed by the bones of dates. Between being born, bonded, and bundled off, whatever they accomplished is gone now. The winds of time have desiccated and scattered all the flesh and muscle of real memories.

Recall that in the Epic of Gilgamesh, the ultimate hope of immortality lies not in a life to come but merely in the fragile memories of survivors. This is certainly a natural sentiment, and perhaps it works for a few generations in closely-knit communities. A Chinese exchange student we had living with us brought pictures of his ancestors going back to the 16th century. But he is clearly an exception to the dark awareness each of us carries: You will not be remembered forever. Almost everyone who has ever lived has been totally forgotten.

It gets worse. If astronomers are right about the death of the sun, everyone *will be* totally forgotten, in a total and irremediable eclipse of stories. "History" dies when *our* story dies. I don't mean the history books. I mean the history as it lives in the backyard chats, the gossip, the congratulatory praises, the nodding agreements, and all the memories we carry in our hearts.

We depend on our memories to help us talk with each other. Each of us acts as a historian specializing in his or her personal biography. Yet, we do not wait for the death of the sun to begin forgetting. Practically everyone complains of having a bad memory. Many of us will suffer from dementia and forget who our friends are and on what street we lived for twenty years. So how is it that we can so dote on stories during our lifetime only to have them eventually slip away? The stories are meaningful, we know that. But their meaningfulness is forgotten.

What is going on here? What is God up to? There has got to be a message here. If we believe that God is kind, logic must conclude that somehow the death of memories is a part of some grander scheme. But how could it be better to forget than to remember? Could it be that despite all the satisfactions of friendship, kinship, and community, we are called to direct our attention elsewhere?

Maybe God gave us leaky memories to help us forgive. Look at children. The reason children don't hold grudges for long is because they can't remember why they felt hurt. Their natural memories would not serve vengeance. And the verb adults use with "grudge" is "nurse," as if you have to keep feeding it or it will die a natural death. The forgiveness that follows forgetfulness seems natural. On the other hand, children just as easily forget gratitude. Gratitude has to be instilled lest they grow up missing birthdays and forgetting to send thank-you notes. A bad memory may make forgiveness easy, but it also makes ingratitude easy. It seems, then, that any divine payoff from our bad memories has both minuses and pluses.

A more sobering explanation of why we are not designed with better memories is that our memory problem forces us to deepen our faith about history. God may well have fashioned us forgetful so that we might turn to faith for assurance that the good is never completely abolished. Our make-up may be such that we eventually wonder about the forward flow of human civilization. God may have given us mediocre memories so that we feel the need for faith in history.

What is faith in history? Jews, Moslems, and Christians hold that God is a God of history. The Bible describes God as choosing a particular nomadic clan, leading them up and down the desert, abandoning them and saving them, chastising them and teaching them, leading them to a promised land and then transforming that promise of real estate into a pledge of a full share in divine life. Islamic and Hebrew texts portray God's dealing with Abraham not as a particularly virtuous or deserving person but precisely as a progenitor of a sanctified people mandated to pass on the faith from one generation to the next. The message is clear: God directs history. God has a plan.

Not everyone believes this, of course. When we read ordinary history books, this plan is far from clear. Hitler and Stalin were responsible for about fifty million deaths, if we include not only the Holocaust but the wars and enslavement camps. Christians in Ireland terrorize each other under the spell of enmities they refuse to forget. Even in our families, we can't help but wonder why, after diligent religious and moral training aimed at passing on the highest values to another generation, some of the kids turn out so bad.

What has happened to this people who regarded themselves as "chosen"? Indeed, what has happened to the rest of the world? What kind of divine plan is this, that lets malice run free? It is scandalous—God's seeming indifference to the fall of entire civilizations, the decay of family life, the dissolution of friendships. It is no wonder that so many people believe that God is interested only in individuals, hoping to save them, where "save" means to lift them free from the ravages of history.

So our faith about history is tested. Does God have a plan for the human race or not? Is the plan merely to lead individuals to religious conversion or is it also to create a God-loving civilization that improves the human condition in the long run? The answers to these questions are hard to come by, particularly when we, with our bad memories, learn so few lessons from history.

Because we lack insight into the workings of history, and because our memories are undependable servants, we must rely on a kind of faith. Faith is not a matter of turning to explanations, either from prophets or from philosophers. Faith relies on simple Yes or No about a proposition. Here the proposition is whether God is interested in the progress of the human race over time. Yes or no? A Yes will drive us deeper into human involvement in politics and economics, with all the moral compromises that come with it. A No will require a deep trust that history will take care of itself while we take our stand on individual virtue. Because we have so little control over the course of history, and because we are so lackadaisical about remembering the lessons of history anyway, we face this question stripped of mere human assurances. This leap of faith in God's providential care over the process of historical development is easily as risky as the leap to believing that God will not abandon any individual to death.

There is a practical conclusion to having faith that history is going somewhere. Even though historians mount volumes of evidence to the contrary, there is a process working in humans that tends to improve the human condition. We called it the Law of Care. That law explains not only the presence of love and community on earth. Recall that this law is about a foward-moving process. It explains the progress of communities in history. Ultimately the Law of Care is about history; and only within history's perspective, about community; and only within community's perspective, about individuals.

This evolving process of history reflects features of God that we easily overlook. Earlier we noted that God is more like a community than an individual. To put it precisely, God is the very love that binds community members together. We suggested that if we want to see God at work, look to human interchange. Now it seems appropriate to consider whether God's fuller image shows itself not in an individual nor in any special community, nor simply in the entire collection of communities distributed over the globe. The fuller image may appear in the development, over time, of a better human race. That is, the image of God quite possibly appears best in the vision of the human community *as it develops historically*.

This compounds the mystery of God. It has been strange enough for believers to imagine a God who is entirely simple and singular yet, at the same time, a plurality. In Christian belief, the life of Jesus and the experience of God's Spirit are understood as God's double gift of the divine self to us. This led to the astonishing conclusion, which took a few hundred years to completely swallow, that God therefore must have a double process intrinsic to the divine nature—an eternally emergent word and an eternally emergent spirit. The word "trinity" represented a mathematical (and, to my mind, misleading) conclusion about the number of entities or realities in God and was merely the code for this belief that God truly shares the divine self with us. As I say, strange enough.

Now, however, since we have realized that we "individuals" are far from solitary entities but rather fulfill the mystery of our personhood only in community, we must push on to keep pace with 19th and 20th century discoveries of the essentially historical character of our existence. If our historical character is not arbitrary but truly essential to our fullest meaning and value, if the Law of Care is about history first and only subsequently about community, then it follows that God has the roots of historicity as part of the divine nature. That is, God's idea of time—history's frame—is not arbitrary. It is drawn from God's character and essence. Where this astonishing conclusion will lead I do not know, except to feel a deepened confidence that when we see God face-to-face, we will see the incredible richness and beauty of human historical process as well. We will see, in a timeless and eternal divinity, time and growth, healing and blossoming, the arc from past to future on which the essence of our freedom depends. In short, our very struggles to accomplish some good and to redeem evil will remain eternally present no matter how "ineffective" their outcomes seemed to us here.

As children, we were taught that God made everything out of nothing. Poof! There's everything! It was like a cosmic magician pulling a universal rabbit from an empty hat. It was totally baffling. As adults, however, we can see that God normally makes things from other things. New ideas, new uses of old tools, new conveniences, new economic arrangements, new political alignments, new people, new families, ... all these take their origins from something else. This is not as baffling as creation out of nothing because we are directly involved in this creativity. But precisely because we are involved, knowing how short-sighted and self-centered beings we are, we easily think that ongoing creativity is continually offset by ongoing self-destruction. While we may not be baffled at how one thing leads to another, we remain deeply uncertain whether the forces of human creativity can really overpower the forces of destruction latent in the hearts of everyone.

So we are left with an act of faith in a historical God. This God is no magician on stage with hidden tricks. This God is part of the audience, relying on the Law of Care among us to produce real miracles.

A CONTEMPLATION OF CARE

We began this chapter by looking at the evidence that the known universe operates by, among many other laws, a law by which successively higher forms eventually emerge. We suggested that since the highest form that has emerged is human caring, we might call this law "The Law of Care." We did so, not so much to give the sciences something to think about, since many scientists already affirm that some such dynamic exists, but rather to use this hypothesis about the universe to ask what God must be like and what role death plays in the human drama. Here and there we drew on the life of Matty Ventresca to pose our questions and illustrate some answers.

Whether or not anyone agrees that a Law of Care is really the best way to formulate human reflections on where the universe may be heading, at least we should keep the evidence in front of us. So I would like to conclude this chapter by inviting you to a highly personal exercise. In this exercise, you will examine very closely what really goes on when you love.

Allow me to speak to you directly. Not as parent to child, but simply as one friend to another. It is time to look at yourself.

So be quiet. Be still.

Gradually put any questions aside. Empty the house of your mind. Escort your personal mental gate crashers out the door.

What you notice is that you start wondering again. Maybe with discipline you can quit analyzing, you can eliminate all concepts and images in a Zen-like inner calm. But before long, you slip from your stillpoint, you return to the busy marketplace, looking for a payoff to this retreat—increased perception, better understanding, wiser judgment.

You can't help it. Despite the high regard in which calm is held, your heart cannot sustain it long. Even the Buddha must deal with questions, more from Buddha than from Buddhists. There is a deep well of wonder in each of us. It lifts our consciousness without asking our permission. It raises questions we did not so much fashion as receive. This passive reception of an inquiring spirit gives each one of us first-hand evidence that, in you, in me, the universe is heading somewhere.

The point is that we experience the Law of Care directly whenever we wonder. And while our *formulation* of that law is meant to give a structural framework for explaining history, community, and personhood, our *experience* of that law can give us important data on God's presence in history, community, and personhood. So let us look more closely at our experience of wonder, understanding, and care.

First of all, wonder is not always impressed by size. If size were really a measure of the importance of things, then a single act of understanding would dwarf Everest. A child's insight into the use of a spoon would be an achievement of such monumental proportions that the drift of continents across our planet's face would appear miniscule.

Wonder is far more impressed by the workings of the mind and heart. Sit in an airport and watch a DC-10 heave to at the jetway. That silver mammoth is entirely controlled by a little pilot you can hardly see through a tiny trapezoidal window above its blunt nose. And, strapped to a little seat, over 98 percent of that pilot's mass comprises various vascular systems and muscular instruments for carrying out orders delivered by the remaining 2 percent, the real control center located behind the pilot's eyes. What really counts for passengers and their luggage is that this puny three-pound lump called a brain had better process data intelligently and size up situations judiciously.

Now look a little closer. To see what is really going on in this pilot's control center, look at something invisible in yourself. Notice how your intelligence and good judgment work best when directed by a healthy love. Isn't this unseen power of love the best conductor of insight and wisdom? Isn't your understanding constipated by a spiteful mood? Doesn't prudence harden into an unreflective steadfastness when you nurse a grudge? Therefore isn't heart the best master of mind, and therefore the best master of the pilot and the best master of the plane? A pilot with a happy home life carries instinctive care for precious freight like a kindly parent. A pilot full of spleen is more likely to throw the plane down on the tarmac.

Love is the most important thing we know of in the universe. Love is "bigger" than anything else, where "bigger" means more important. And it is going on now. In you.

What's more, *your* love is absolutely unique. No one else loves whom and what you love, nor with the particular depth of love that you bear. In you the universe is absolutely specialized. Without you and the particular way you love, your immediate surroundings would be different. These differences would ripple out, affecting eventually everything. The future of everything depends on you and your love.

If you feel in any way special on account of these reflections, this is good. You are absolutely special. A cosmic VIP. Not because you give love; more because you are receiving the power to love. Your wonder—that spontaneous care in your heart, the tide of love that carries you wherever you go—is a gift pouring out from God into your heart.

You sometimes doubt that God loves you. This is natural. Not because you are unlovable but because none of us easily recognizes what may be love when it comes our way. A look at the evidence can help, however. The love with which you love is God's loving gift to you. That rising in your heart is God's kind doting on you. We wouldn't give a damn about God if God had not already loved us—because giving a damn is God's gift of love.

On those days when you doubt your worth, you may try to remember that God loves you. Good luck. Normally the psyche needs a little proof, not a dry dogma. A better strategy is to notice the burgeoning of your wonder inside, that longing for understanding, that struggle to tell right from wrong, and your efforts to act on your convictions. Look at how frustrated you are in loving others. You'd never be frustrated if God were not flooding your heart with love, pouring it into every available corner like someone obsessed with sharing everything with you. In other words, look first at how you love and discover there the constant evidence that you are loved.

We should use a yellow felt marker in our minds to highlight the main point about love. God's love for us is, in one crucial respect, completely different from our love for each other. In my love for you and yours for me, we are inspired to give gifts to each other, giving, as far as we can, our very selves. But I do not give you your love for me. You may be the object of my love, but you are not its source. You may be the reason I want to direct my love to you. But before I directed it, I received that power to love. God, however, is the source of all our loves and, more to the point, the source of everything in us that longs for the most beautiful, the most worthwhile, the best—in short, our love for God.

This reminds me of a November years ago when my mother lost her favorite pair of scissors. She looked for weeks without success. Come Christmas, my brother Bob, about five-years-old then, had a scissors-shaped present sitting under the Christmas tree for my mother. She was delighted that he would be so thoughtful although she was sure that one of the older kids bought the new scissors for him to give her. But no one had. As she was unwrapping it, Bob said, "I knew you really needed it." Sure enough, it was a pair of scissors. But not a *new* pair. It was the "lost" pair that he had stolen from her sewing drawer in order to give her something she really would be happy to receive!

When we love God, we act as though the love was ours to give. But, really, and this is the essential difference between loving God and loving each other, that love came from God in the first place. Like my brother Bob, we give only what we have first received.

There's still more (Are you with me?) God does nothing shoddy. If God intends to love us, that love will go all the way. Just as in human love we die to our isolated consciousness for the sake of a common consciousness, so God "dies" to an isolated self-presence for the sake of a common consciousness with us. In the First Letter of John it says, "God *is* love. Whoever abides in love abides in God."

In other words, this special feeling we experience when we realize (1) that God loves us and (2) that God showers love-power upon us, is a result of God living in us. "You have in you one who is greater than anyone in the world," it says in the First Letter of John. God is spirit, and this spirit, being free to reside in whatever matter it chooses, takes up residence in us as love. The waves of love we experience in our everyday lives give us personalized and concrete evidence that God wants nothing more than to give the divine self to us without reserve.

As we grow into adulthood, it occurs to us that life is short. We cannot carry out everything that our love would like to do. But because it is not originally our love, because our aching love is a love of a God who aches to make love complete, because we are stewards of our love and not its owners, we have to bow to love's authority and let it have its way with us in our latter years.

Death is God's patience running out. Time now for God to carry us along in perfect love. Although we wish we could hang around a while longer to carry out our love-plans, God's love-plans carry *us* out, carry us to love's completion, an embrace for which everything in us aches yet which nothing in us adequately imagines.

CHAPTER 5
Voices of Redemption

Since when does coming "back" to life
Redeem what went before?
What counts is going 'on' to life:
New me, new us, and more.

When I first saw the marker where Matty's ashes are buried, I felt for a boy who lost his life. He lived for nine years, and now he is dead. This is how we usually envision life and death. First life, then death. He was there, now he's not.

But later I met his family and learned what his life was about—his love for lizards, flying kites on sunny days, and especially the love Matty gave his family, in the uninhibited fullness of innocence. I began to realize that Matty's life was not just breath and heartbeats, a life that ends where death begins, a life defined by medicine. Opposing life and death like this trivializes the reality. On the one hand, death accompanied Matty's life; he lived more richly because he befriended death. On the other, Matty has not completely died; his face and smile continue to teach about patience, and hope, and deep trust despite life's setbacks. His family has been permanently marked by the life he shared with them. So life is not the opposite of death. There's an overlap. The abiding concern we have for life is not to lengthen it and put off death as far as possible, although at times this seems to be the case. Ordinarily our concern is to deepen our life, make today richer, uncover dimensions we have not yet experienced.

The irony is that we deepen life by allowing certain kinds of death to enrich our everyday living. We "die" to desires for revenge. We "die" to the urge to steal. We "die" to harboring lies in our hearts. We can think of life as booty of a war, the result of a struggle. We don't simply "live" life. We fight for it against forces that could ruin us. The tiny seeds of immortality in our souls sprout in doing what is good, in kindness and love toward others. Our immortality is inextricably linked with our morality, a morality we have to nourish in an environment clanging with contradictory messages about good and bad. We have to find a humane outcome to situations where everyone, including ourselves, has acted with greed or spite.

No doubt Matty had made some things worse and other things better. He was not perfect. But we should not measure the value of his life by some calculation of his net contribution. If life were a matter of doing more good things than bad, then God is just an accountant with a balance sheet. But if God is a lover of the good, and if God lives *in* us to bring about that good, then besides just the *doing* of good, there is the *undoing* of the bad. Besides ethical living, there is redemption of what is unethical. Besides human creativity bringing progress, there is divine care bringing healing.

All of us are born into situations that are a mixture of good and bad. The ways our parents treat each other are not 100 percent wonderful. The ways our cities are organized are not 100 percent good ideas. The education we received is not 100 percent true. We arrive here with a heart that naturally seeks the good but in a situation that is a jumble of good and bad. The greater percentage of bad, the more difficult for even the best of hearts to know what may be good. It is this redemptive side of moral living, not the creative, that most clearly requires some kind of death.

Of course, there are hundreds of opinions about redeeming bad situations. Some people preach getting even. Some justify killing their enemies. Others stump for creative enterprises that will avoid old mistakes. Still others believe that it is up to authorities to guide the ordinary person because personal inspirations are the enemies of good order.

How should bad situations be redeemed? In this chapter, we will look at some of these voices of redemption. Our aim is to understand the subtle way in which death—the moral deaths required by authenticity—is the path to redeeming situations gone awry. At the same time we will fill out a picture of God as redeemer that may replace less appropriate pictures of God as an accountant.

THE SHERIFF'S VOICE

Westerns—the movies—feed on two different threats to life. The minor threat comes from nature and sets the scene for the major threat, which is the bad guy. Against a big sky background of settlers struggling to stay alive under the ravages of drought and disease, in rides the good guy. He's the tall cowboy, eyes shaded under a white hat, and lightning on the draw. When he shoots half a dozen low-lifes, we all cheer. Evil has been overcome. It's Western morality at its finest. Redeem by killing the bad guy. No stray bullet ever kills a horse, obviously, since that would violate our deep reverence for life.

A steady diet of these movies makes it difficult to notice that the death at life's end is not necessarily the worst thing that can happen to us. The cowboy shoot-'em-dead strategy for dealing with evil assumes that death is the ultimate penalty to pay for being a bad guy. The notion that death is the worst thing pervades not only the Westerns but most crime dramas today.

We may laugh off their superficiality, but if we don't read novels and see movies with more depth, we won't think much about how good and evil have roots within everyone, sheriff and bandit alike. These Western-style movies and books pay no mind to the struggles of conscience or to the self-denial that comes with taking responsibility. It is these inner struggles that threaten life. Outer threats such as hurricanes and earthquakes, disease and poverty, muggers and rapists, do not, by themselves, make us who we are. They may shorten our lives or cause us great stress, but they only set the stage for the inner struggle to act with integrity, responsibility, intelligence, and care. These struggles of conscience pose a far more subtle threat because they actually require some measure of death to maintain the core of life. Because these interior battles require their own kind of deaths, we cannot depict them in the typical Western terms of life-versus-death. The kind of death they require is the death of something in the heart. It's a matter of life *through* death.

Here, someone might say, "Oh, you're just speaking metaphorically. That's a kind of *moral* death. Real death is when you stop breathing, period." Really? Is that what "real death" is? Are all the physical deaths we see in Westerns "really" death?

Certainly, the end of our biological lives is something real. But saying it is real is only one step toward understanding what it means. The meaning of our physical deaths lies in the realm of our care for each other. Here is where we mourn the loss of our loved ones and, at the same time, bear in memory the unique poignancy of their particular lives. Here is where, for the people who have died, there is no more chance to reinterpret their past, no more opportunity to reconsider how they divided good from bad in their lives. Here is where all the provisional meanings borne by the moral deaths they experienced during their lifetimes become permanent. The quietus of physical death is the silence of a judge who has spoken the verdict.

I am not speaking of some "last judgment" by God in some imaginary future in an afterlife. I'm speaking of the verdict that dying persons pass on themselves as they assess how they have lived. I'm speaking of the verdict that all living persons pass on themselves throughout life. I'm speaking of the familiar judgment we pass on ourselves that we either have given up the fight or we are still fighting to maintain our integrity. And if we have given up this fight, then we experience the death of our spirits that would rather fight. If we are fighting to maintain our integrity, then we experience the death of many desires for revenge and self-gain. For the sake of discussion, let us call these two kinds of death "mortal" and "transforming."

"Mortal death" occurs not in an instant but rather through a long string of choices. It forms like cooling lava, taking shape as these choices gel into a habit, and a habit hardens into a commitment to serving self over others no matter what the cost. It is the death that gradually encases the person who hoards energies, information, assistance, the kind word, the smile, the hand. By becoming detached from opportunities to care, the mortally sick person must bung the heart lest it inadvertently release an outpouring of compassion.

Like many organisms destined for extinction, this person sets up routines that are both self-destructive and progressively immune to the healing interventions of others. Their routines result from having withdrawn from the community and from the store of wisdom that the community has achieved painstakingly over time. It appears that to the extent anyone disengages from the community for the express purpose of borrowing its resources without donating any in return, he or she simultaneously destroys the very internal elements that are necessary for the making of a genuine individual.

Paradoxically, mortal deaths are the result of inner *failures* to kill—the failure to suppress hatred, the failure to kill ideas that serve the self over others, the failure to strangle those voices of fear that prevent one from speaking up and acting appropriately. Moral wimps may not deliberately kill their consciences, but by failing to defend themselves against the heart's true enemy, they leave their consciences unprotected. They truly die.

"Transforming death" likewise forms slowly through a series of choices, but in these choices it is we who do the killing—all the kills we have carried out against the forces of hatred, egotism, and cowardice as they gathered in our hearts or that others have urged upon us. We commit murder like this hundreds of times a day.

Fortunately, a familiar feature of the Law of Care—which always has been latent in the potentialities of evolution—is that those who *give* care will also *receive* it. It is the nature of transforming deaths to keep us in touch with people who support us in life's struggle. So, transforming deaths keep our hearts healthy. They allow us to direct our care to those around us and, by so doing, open us to experience care coming our way.

The physical death at the last minute of our lives can therefore bear only one of two opposite meanings. People living in mortal death come to a final and terrible end when their hearts give out. Everything they gathered will be taken away; having planted nothing, they die fruitless. It is no wonder they should fear, deny, avoid, and delay their death. On the other hand, people living in transforming death set their lives before God on that day with deep calm. Most of what they planted will live on in those they cared for. Death is nothing new to them. Experience has taught them that death usually contains the seeds of life and that there is no magnificence to life without it. If we lived in "transforming deaths," then our death is a symbol of our final and irrevocable gift of self to the welfare of those we love.

In recent years, physicists and economists have reluctantly accepted the unsettling notion of "indeterminacy" in nature and economics. Physicists will never determine both the speed and the location of an electron simultaneously. Economists will never predict the cycles of economics, which they once described as unbendable iron. Indeterminacy also extends to human death. We cannot determine ahead of time whether any individual's death will be mortal or transforming. When we die, our death draws its reality from our life. If we lived in "mortal deaths," hoarding and hating, then our physical death is our final and irrevocable separation from the human family. The family would have fared better without us. If we lived in "transforming deaths," killing off bad inspirations, then our physical death is our final and irrevocable joining of the human family.

In reality, then—in hard, implacable reality—the good guys die a very different death than the bad guys. But you don't change the death of the bad guys by shooting them. Redemption of evil cannot come about by killing. There was wisdom in Jesus' comparison of redemption to separating weeds from wheat: be careful lest you uproot the wheat as well. Redemption is a slow, tedious process. You do it gradually, patiently, with kindness and education. The earlier you start the better, since the character of one's death takes a long time to shape.

We can summarize the lesson here in a Western mode: On those days when you still feel the itch to leap onto your horse and ride out after those dirty, low-down, sneaky sidewinders, you can skip the horse. The bad guys are in your heart, sheriff.

THE VOICE OF THE FANS

When police chased Oreanthal Simpson to arrest him in connection with the killing of his wife and her friend, millions of Americans saw him on TV in his white Bronco, sailing past side streets like yard-lines. The public's fascination with this story resulted from an inability to sort out three contradictory emotions that were being broadcast that day. One, people on roadsides and overpasses were cheering him on, as if he were still a halfback zipping between linebackers. Two, the police were expressing anxiety that Mr. Simpson might take his own life, so that even after they jailed him, they posted guards on a "suicide watch." Three, prosecutors were noting that because of "special circumstances," meaning the especially cruel hacking received by the two victims, Simpson could be subject to the death penalty.

Simpson was found not guilty by one court and guilty by another. Yet, looking back on it all, it did seem ironical that the main benefit of the "suicide watch" might be to save him for *our* killing. We also protect admitted killers on death row from killing themselves. Society forbids you to take your own life, but it can and will take your life from you, given the right circumstances. Could someone please explain this to me?

The prosecution had decided not to seek the death penalty anyway. The stated reason was that a jury would be much more reluctant to convict a famous person if conviction meant death. This gives us an interesting insight into what Americans think about killing someone famous. Simpson's persona carried a force in people's minds that far outweighed the expertise of his lawyers and their defense that the evidence may have been planted. We can't kill him because he did fantastic things for football, he entertained us, he got rich and famous. We can't kill him, well, just because he's "O.J."

We prefer our killers to be unknown. These we can march off to the gas chamber. It makes no difference to us whether a person succeeded in *resisting* evildoing for decades or spent dozens of years raising a family. The real test of whether we kill someone is how much we feel the person is not part of the American community. Unfortunately, that depends on publicity, not character. You are not really a full person in the United States until you are widely known. The most financially successful artists are usually hum-drum in their studios but wizards in the marketplace. Every week, famous and already-wealthy TV evangelists receive hundreds of ten-dollar checks from people less well-off and far less famous. If someone wins the lottery and wishes to remain anonymous, the rest of us feel cheated—not because we didn't win but because we expect that the rich *should* be famous.

The truth is, we Americans do *not* believe in capital punishment. Not for real persons. We just don't think many of us get to be real. Lucky for Oreanthal, he got to be a real person, unlike the rest of us nobodies.

According to most religions, everyone is created equal and everyone is equally under God's rule. God's dominion levels humanity, mainly through the crucible of death. This is the plain belief of religious people everywhere. Among Muslims, the dominant belief is that each person must die and that one's subsequent fate depends on what angels have recorded in the books of good and bad deeds. Moreover, Muslims are encouraged to emulate the Sufis in the way they anticipate death while still alive. The Sufis lived an otherworldly existence through dying to oneself, of leaving behind one's worldly cares, and of focusing on Allah above all. Although Westerners today generally regard Islam as a threat to its ways, Muhammad himself counseled his followers that they should erase distinctions between themselves and Arabs, and, indeed, between any black and white.

Throughout the Hebrew scriptures, God is constantly adjusting Jewish assumptions of who is a real person. God typically chooses the unlikely to humble the proud. Isaac was the surprise birth. Jacob robbed Esau of his birthright. David was a last-born, grandson of a Moab. Moses was lucky to be found in a marsh, by a princess, no less. Amos tended sheep.

In that vein, the New Testament shows Jesus as being raised in a culture that did not treat everyone as equal. It states that Jesus was from Nazareth, about which people said, "What good can come from there?" But Jesus himself treated each person as special. The woman at the well, the widow from Naim, the man born blind, the woman with a hemorrhage, the man beset by demons—we can't help noticing how *unknown* all these people are. Jesus always seemed to interrupt the flow of things to attend to the nobodies, often to the chagrin of his disciples who, if they really were disciples, were supposed to be taking notes. He reached across the iron boundaries of gender, of race, of social class, and of health that kept people in their place. It was not because of divine knowledge that Jesus never asked anyone's name. (Indeed, an intelligent compassion knows how names—"Son of Timaeus" and "Joseph of Arimathaea"—tend to lock people into social roles.) Even after he cures them, he lets them walk out of the gospel story without becoming famous. He does not even require faith on their part beforehand. Of the woman accused of adultery, Jesus didn't require faith from her *before* shaming her accusers into dropping their stones. It seemed enough for him to hope that her faith would blossom *after* experiencing God's forgiveness.

The message here is simple: Death homogenizes us. Our social categories are ultimately shallow conventions. People of faith see this and regard every person as a real person, regardless of titles or possessions and regardless of wickedness and shame. Real faith does not even exalt earnest do-gooders over repentant sinners. Even people without any apparent faith are regarded as real persons, whether or not they care little for notoriety.

Let us return to the courtroom where, in many states, killing is legal. Picture the family of a man who has been killed. Picture them sitting there as the jury finds his killer guilty. And listen to the judge sentence the killer to die by lethal injection. What happens to that family then? The family must go on without the man they love—a sentence that, to their mind, far outweighs the capital punishment his killer will receive. Some members may well tell themselves that while his killer's death will give them no satisfaction, it is a simple matter of justice that he die. Others may admit that there is some measure of vengeful satisfaction here. The tragedy here is now multiplied because these family members will think of terminating a life as one way to solve problems. Not that they justify senseless murder, but society has told them that some problems can be solved only be eliminating a person.

Eliminating someone now becomes a moral option. When a company is downsizing, eliminating people becomes just a little easier than relocating them or assisting them in finding work elsewhere. When an aging widow sees her savings rapidly going to a nursing home, she more easily thinks of eliminating herself so that her children will have some inheritance. When teenage gangs run into trouble with rival gangs, they more quickly think of guns as problem solvers. Now the murdered man's family becomes victimized by what society considers to be a solution to their problem. After all the financial and sociological arguments against capital punishment have run their course, there remains the sobering argument that it is the outraged society that pays a high price. One evil has generated another by proliferating the idea that eliminating people can eliminate problems.

There is no redemption of this man's murder here because redemption means bringing good out of evil. The only genuine redemption is to allow the killer to live. It makes for a strong message to him about the sanctity of life. And even if he spends the rest of his days unrepentant, even if he carries a hatred of society to his grave, at least the judge, jury, witnesses, and family and friends of the murdered man have put an end to the proliferation of the killer's most unholy way of solving problems.

THE LANGUAGE OF REDEMPTION

"Dead."

"Dead."

"Dead."

Aunt Donna is going through her coupons, pitching the old ones out. About six million coupons "die" in the United States every day, while, during the same day, only six thousand people die.

It's curious how we so easily use this word about everyday things. Why wouldn't we reserve "die" to something only humans do, or at least have a special word for how humans do it? Sometimes we say coupons "expire." They have "expiration dates." Fine, but it is really the same as "died." *Expire* refers to the last breath of a living person. Etymologically it means "spirit going out."

We can find "death" in the most mundane things. When we have to accomplish something by a certain time, we say we have a "deadline" to meet. Presumably this means that something dies if we don't accomplish it by the time limit. Many of the things around us are time's victims too. Our batteries die. Our plants die. It appears that time—

and the limited amount of it—is what everything has in common. Time appears to be moving everything along to extinction, to failure, to an end.

What is more, the time we share is not something neutral. We consider time as a measure of productivity. Anything that doesn't produce work we call "dead." An electrician calls a wire "dead." Any *person* that doesn't work we call "dead weight." Any one who doesn't pay debts is a "deadbeat." What is frightening about this connection between death and production is that it then becomes too easy to regard the elderly and handicapped as without any worth alive. They're practically dead anyway—where *practically* now means far more than *in the practical order of things*; it now means *in any conceivably worthwhile respect*. If you are not of any practical use, you are "practically dead." Time seems to have carried you to your deadline. You have expired.

We fight the clock as if life were mainly a matter of delivering some commodity. We work faster and harder. When we spend a few leisure hours we say we have been "killing" time. This is a remarkable notion. It means that "live" time is productive time, and when we're not productive, we've killed time. Actually, most of us kill time on purpose because we resent the equation of time and accomplishment. Killing time is our temporary revolt against an artificial measure of our worth.

In an interesting juxtaposition of terms, notice what we do when we put coupons to use before they die: we *redeem* them. Sometimes we say "redeem" when we use our time productively: "At least we can redeem the time remaining if we get down to business."

The sales departments of the world have raided the lexicon of theology and stolen fine words like "die" and "redeem" for mercantile purposes. So we should at least watch our language. Although it is useless to try to restrict familiar words to their deeper meanings, we can at least remind each other of these deeper meanings. Death is not about ending productivity. And redemption is not about coupons or the efficient use of time.

REDEMPTION IS ABOUT TROUBLE

We have seen that mortality is about morality, that death is about living, that how we end life depends on how well or poorly we lived it. We have seen that any final meaning of my life is not some arithmetic sum of positives and negatives. A better mathematical analogy might be an integral calculus in which later operations can integrate earlier ones. That is, while I am alive, I can put a better light on my past by becoming a better person. Old mistakes are provisional, after all, just as old successes can be steps on a road ending in failure. But once I am dead, all is in place. I can no longer say the memorable word or do the remarkable deed that will lead everyone to reconsider what they thought of me. My life is then what it will always have been. I can no longer exercise any free and responsible control. I can no longer change my mind, my attitudes, my self.

This view makes the idea of redemption more clear. Just as death is about morality, so "redemption" is about trouble—what trouble really is and how I might be snatched out of it while I'm alive. We are all mired in trouble, some of it our own doing, but most of it the doing of others. However, it is no small thing to recognize what that trouble really is. Just as there are dozens of opposing opinions about morality, so there are dozens of opposing opinions about trouble. For some, trouble is essentially the breaking of any rule; for others it is being rule-bound. For some, trouble is failure to trust in God and in the goodness of other people; for others it is failing to put demands on God and being suspicious of other people. For some, trouble comes when you fail to move with the changing times; for others, change itself spells trouble. Being mixed-up about what real trouble is, we are going to be mixed-up about what redemption is.

One thing redemption is *not* about is "fixing." You fix something that is broken. You restore it to its original functioning. Everybody involved is happy that things have returned to normal. A football coach may say the team "redeemed" last year's poor win-loss record by wholloping every team in sight, but they might better have said they "fixed" the situation.

In John the Evangelist's story of Jesus raising Lazarus, we can see the profound difference between *fixing* and *redeeming*. When Jesus brought Lazarus back to life, he "fixed" a problem. Lazarus came back to what he was. He would eventually die again. (It is good to remember here that John's stories were directed to people who already had a profound religious sensibility. Right from the start, his hearers were on the lookout for the deeper meaning to the raising of Lazarus story. Because they were people who were keenly aware of the mystery of God in ordinary life—in my opinion far more than we are today—they saw that the raising of a dead man was only a vague pointer to the profound resurrection of the human race embodied in the person of Jesus.)

Beneath that surface layer of a human coming back to life, John wanted to symbolize the profound mystery of the resurrected life—which is something else altogether. John's point seems to be that just as on an earthly plane Jesus raised Lazarus to earthly life, so on a divine plane, God would raise Jesus to divine life. The difference is that when God raised Jesus in the resurrection, all humankind was "redeemed." Jesus did not come back to what he was. Something new had occurred. Everybody was turned upside down because Jesus did not take up sword against sword. He let the religious jealousy of the pharisees and the madness of mob frenzy do their worst to him rather than compromise what love moved him to do. He prayed God would forgive those who were taking his life. Sin was no longer the last word on human destiny. Forgiveness became the last word.

It appears, then, that it is the nature of life, particularly human life, that its value is enhanced when people follow the dictates of their hearts rather than their fear of death, even if it means a life shortened through the stupidity, envy, or pride of others. Real trouble, in other words, lies not in death but in succumbing to the fear of death.

Nor is true redemption the same as that vastly overrated human gift we call "creativity." I define creativity as the ability to see that everything is possibly something else. A coat hanger is a locked-car unlocker. Two plastic bags are boots in unexpected rainy weather. Bicycle handlebars are horns on a sculpture of a longhorn steer. Even a shy teenager can amazingly become a thundering Othello when decked out in costume and put on stage. But creativity also has its dark side. The coat hanger may help someone steal your car. A con artist is still wonderfully creative even when an old person's savings are wiped out in some clever scam.

In true redeeming, we do not apply an astute insight that makes a good situation better. Nor do we exercise creativity. That is, we do not make something into something else. On the contrary, redemption honors the actual, concrete meaning of a person or situation by conferring a new worth on what already exists. It doesn't look for a new reality to replace the old. Essentially, redeeming is about transforming bad into good. It means beating malice through forgiveness. We face a situation full of irrationalities and get people to find common ground rather than punish those responsible. We mysteriously produce good out of evil.

True redemptions are unlike lofty creativity. Everyone applauds creative inventions that benefit them; they happily praise the creative person. But when a situation is "redeemed," everybody involved has been profoundly disturbed. Take the family of a man who acknowledges his alcoholism and does something about it. He won't be the same full-of-promises optimist anymore. His wife and kids will not be completely pleased with genuine sobriety when they see it. The roles they played in the addiction-scripted home will be cancelled. As he follows through breaking off his relationship with the bottle, they will have to drop their roles and draw more directly from their hearts.

Perhaps we can keep these things in mind if we try to use this meaning of "redeem" in our conversation. At a minimum, watching our language might remind us to keep our eyes open to the web of irrationalities in which our society is entangled. At a maximum, we can hope that an awareness of the need for redemption in everyday situations will prepare us to repay evil with good, to turn the other cheek, to walk the second mile. We might remember that mere cleverness will not do. At work, when choosing employees or colleagues, although we rank creativity higher than the ability to fix, we might rank the ability to redeem higher than mere creativity.

THE REDEEMING WORD

To a biologist, life is the opposite of death, where death is nothing more than the breakdown of cells, organisms, and various nutritional and reproductive systems. Until recently, medical doctors have tended to define life in the same way, directing their best efforts toward maintaining physical life as long as possible. They have been wonderfully successful, but the publicity earned by their successes said to the general public, "The longer you live, the better." People had the impression from these respected professionals that the best life is the longest life. The idea that the Grim Reaper could be held at bay was greeted with optimism.

Now we hear different voices. For many terminally ill people, this extension of life only prolonged their physical agony, their worries about paying medical bills, and their guilt at being a continuing burden on their families. The very presumption that life ought to be extended has cast a dark shadow on old age. To most people, being old and being worthless are the same thing. Have you noticed people saying recently, "That gets old"?

Ironically, it was the terminal illness of a rather young woman that raised a new question in the mind of the general public about whether a lengthened life may actually be less valuable than a shortened one. During the 1970s, Karen Ann Quinlan overdosed on a mixture of alcohol and tranquilizers and fell into an irreversible coma. Her life was sustained—or, more to the point, extended—by a ventilator and an intravenous feeding tube. Eventually her parents fought the current laws and moral standards and were allowed to withdraw her artificial life supports. Although she continued living for several more years (perhaps because they gradually weaned her from the ventilator rather than stopping it all at once), her parents made the decision to let her die.

In a crucially important respect, Karen Ann was not alone. She represented the growing number of people who were being kept alive by the decisions of medical professionals who were unprepared to consider the deeper issue of what being kept "alive" really means for a human.

Karen Ann's family reacted against the standard medical protocols that kept such decisions in the hands of doctors alone. To a great extent because of her family's leadership, most Americans today take some steps regarding their wishes about how they are to die. This is a new phenomenon, quite unlike ways of planning one's death that we are already familiar with. For example, people contemplating suicide think of death as a high price to pay to end their misery. Or martyrs regard death as a high price to pay, but worth it for some noble cause. But most of us now worry about *not* dying and lingering instead on the cliff edge of death, far from the sweet fields of ordinary life. When we imagine ourselves as terminally ill, death is not a high price to pay; it is rather an *end* to paying high prices—the financial, emotional, and physical high prices. In these extremities, our death is not some abhorrent destruction; it is a welcomed guest.

Certainly, there is something tragic about Karen Ann's life being cut short. Unlike the very elderly, whose powers are failing, everything in Karen Ann was geared to live on, until she foolishly mixed tranquilizers and alcohol. Then nature followed its unbreakable rules and dropped her into a deep coma. Nobody is exempt from this humiliation at the hands of nature. Tragic though this was, it alerted many to the need for a new notion of "life" that the medical profession ought to embrace, a notion that takes its meaning from human values, not from biology alone. That notion is now commonly referred to as "quality of life." Hospital and hospice ethics committees now weigh end-of-life decisions in terms of "quality-life-years," not just years.

Although the Quinlan case has been highly-publicized in the literature of medical ethics, it raises a lesser-recognized issue in how we think God normally talks to us. We often think of "revelation" as some voice out of the sky, or some deep meaning in sacred scriptures. But there is also "revelation" from God in our normal lives. The issue here is how God usually reveals the divine will about what the most ethical behavior may be in the difficult situations we encounter every day.

For many people, the issue is already settled: God simply does not reveal the divine will to individuals. We have been given general laws, and we have the examples of good people to show us what virtuous conduct is, but there is no way to know God's thoughts about individuals. Maybe God has no such thoughts. On the other hand, religious people everywhere find themselves praying for light in their particular situation, asking for guidance to help them through very specific troubles. They presume that among all the options available, one is objectively the best—the one God sees. Although they seldom experience overwhelming certitude about God's will, they act on the presumption that God knows what is best and wills it to come to pass in us as we sort out our options. So let us look more closely at how religious people regard God's will. Let us ask this question: How does God talk to people?

Many religions portray God as speaking in words through some book or prophet. Islam is a prime example, with its focus on Muhammad and the Koran. So is much of Christianity, beginning with the community for whom Matthew wrote his gospel. (Matthew suppresses practically all mention of the Holy Spirit in favor of the words of church authorities appointed by Jesus. He clearly thinks God prefers to speak through official mouthpieces.)

Yet many other religions portray God as speaking wordlessly in each person's innermost heart. This is a core inspiration in Protestantism. The "protest" in Protestantism, after all, was against the authoritarianism of Roman Christianity and an attempt to bring personal inspiration by God back into the picture. We can see this tendency in those charismatic groups that lean against authority rather than toward it—a tendency we can see in the Gospel of John. We can see it in a modified fashion in those sectarian, antisocial fringe groups that demand total dedication to a charismatic leader. Although they seem to preach following the rules, they ultimately are based not on any list of rules but on the mind of the leader. Whatever the leader says, God says, and only the leader gets the divine inspirations. To some extent, this religious individualism shows in the anti-dogmatic style of both conservative Unitarian churches and the libertine, freestyle, eclectic enthusiasms of searchers one imagines are found mainly in California.

What Karen Ann Quinlan's tragedy reveals is that for new moral issues, neither book, leader, nor conscience alone provide much reliable revelation. The experience of the Quinlan family is a story with a message, namely, that we ordinarily learn the will of God where people act conscientiously. Without any knowledge or collaboration on her part, Karen Ann's tragedy provided the palpable reason for her parents to proclaim to the world that prolonging a merely vegetative life is not worthwhile. They were not trying convert others; they only wanted to solve their own problems. But neither can they avoid being a kind of "word" to others. It is not some conceptual word which they speak. Nor is it a word tailored to some clientele. This word is their original, real-life, moral struggle with right and wrong. In this word others hear a word of integrity and a statement on the relative values of suffering and companionship—a word on life.

The human race always achieves whatever moral progress it has made through a process like this. People are not converted by talk. Talk tends to create *fans*, while example usually fosters authentic *living*. When we feel a sense of company with those whose authenticity is challenged by some moral dilemma, we begin to act differently. Of course, we want the people we admire to talk. We want to write down what they say. But what we ultimately want is to *live* at the depth that they do.

So this seems to be the ordinary way in which God speaks to us. God does not usually reveal the divine will in mystical communications. The divine will is not first delivered through a rule or through someone's theory. God seems to have so arranged things that the new moral challenges presented by a developing technology are met when somebody takes action. Action is what convinces us. It is only following upon such action that we codify the rules, write the laws, and praise the lives of the virtuous. The laws, the books, and the stories about our charismatic leaders are our necessary but insufficient attempts to convey moral viewpoints to one another and to our children.

With this view of revelation in mind, I believe the traditional Christian belief in Jesus can be expressed in a way less dogmatic and more attractive to people who have never heard of Jesus. It may also be palatable to those who have been scandalized—justifiably—at the behavior of some who call themselves "Christians."

Where old Christian creeds proclaim Jesus Christ is the "Son" of God and, mysteriously, is truly God, newer, more ecumenically-minded creeds might proclaim Jesus as God's "word." I mean this is the same sense Karen Ann Quinlan is, to a lesser degree, a "word" of God. This "word" is a revelation of ultimate values to be found in historical events, in the lives of real people, in the happenings of a people doing their best in this place at this time.

Jesus wrote no laws and had a far briefer public speaking career than most prophets. His disciples were not particularly anxious to write down everything he said and did. It was only after thirty years had passed that the Gospels began to be written, and the first accounts on which the Gospels are based were accounts of his passion and death, not recordings of his sermons and descriptions of his miracles. To the first disciples, God was speaking through Jesus' actions. Preeminently, Jesus' passion and death revealed that it is better to suffer evil than to do evil. His public life revealed that, in God's eyes, everyone is of equal dignity.

In this perspective, the "word" of God is less a noun, more a verb. It is a person living a human life. To be more specific, it is a word of *example* and a word of *engagement*. Karen Ann and her parents have been an example for others who must make end-of-life decisions; they have also provided some sense of company with people facing these difficult choices. Jesus was a word that *reveals* what God is really like and an *engagement* with subsequent history—a word *par excellence*. Jesus is God "speaking" the divine self in the grammar of flesh and blood. The worth of Jesus is not locked somehow in a divine "nature" or "sonship." His worth lies in how he connects with us, how he communicates to us, how God "speaks a word" to us that reveals what is good and true, and draws us to honor it in practice.

This "word on life" doesn't arrive sheerly from outside of us. Just as a spoken word is just noise unless someone hears and understands, so God's word in Jesus or in any other religious leader will literally mean nothing unless it means something to *someone*. And in that someone, there first has to be a readiness, a wonder, a question, a seeking in the people who need this word. This prior receptiveness to God's word on life is what many religions call the Holy Spirit. Perhaps a better term in this context is a Welcoming Spirit, since the thirst for a word on life is a search ready to welcome whatever brings clarity, assurance, conviction, and comfort.

I have been referring to Jesus of Nazareth by way of example, preëminent though it be. I mean to illustrate how God's word to us is simultaneously external and internal. Externally, God speaks through history, in the histories of all good women and men. Yet, as any high school history teacher will remind us, no history is taught where students are distracted. God's word in history is heard only where people already want to hear. History comes alive in the present only where the human spirit speaks the word, "Come!" Then the word of history and the word of hearts are one, as it were. God's word on life has been uttered and heard.

When this happens, people do not experience "certitude" about God's will. Such an expression is misleading. It portrays a human mind intellectually ascertaining a factual account of God's state of mind. But questions about how to be fully human are not questions of fact. They are questions of value. The best we can achieve is a kind of conviction, not a certitude, and the state of conviction requires a measure of personal commitment quite unnecessary to the state of certitude. This conviction, in turn, is impossible in practice without the experience of some assurance of divine company in taking the step. Pilgrims without maps, we can commit ourselves to the road if we trust that God walks with us.

If this is how God talks to us, then we come face to face with a strange attitude in God. God seems to prefer that we draw on general rules and examples drawn from history, but that in the application of those lessons, we add some measure of personal risk regarding their applicability to the situation at hand. That additional measure is our contribution to history. Even if we later prove to have made a terrible moral error, God seems to prefer that at least we made the attempt. At a minimum, our experience falls into the category of "what to avoid in the future" in our common, ongoing search for what makes for a genuinely good life. At a maximum, however, our experience is an act of co-creation with God. What is good in this situation was heretofore known to no one, and certainly done by no one. And we have done it. By taking this moral leap, we not only act on what God has "spoken" to us, we also become an example, part of God's historical word to those around us whose hearts are crying, "Come!"

The Ventrescas took a risk, a risk that would make a Billy Graham hesitate. By adopting Matty, they redeemed an otherwise terrible situation. Their risk was costly, hard on their family life and hard on their individual emotions. We even have to say that the justification of their risk lay not in Matty's beautiful disposition, as if this was a "reward" from God. Had Matty turned out to be a raging psychotic, their decision to adopt would be no less good. Happy outcomes are not the proof of God at work. The proof of God at work is people listening to their best selves, listening to their inspirations, and acting upon them. Where this occurs, God's Spiritual Word moves people, and these people become God's Historical Word for all to hear.

CHAPTER 6
Walking in the Shadow of Death

Like pond-bound fish under global vaults of air,
speckled by beams from up beyond our sight,
whence luster menaces yet entices,
what shall we make of the light?

The Scottish philosopher John Macmurray held the opinion that intelligent people always keep one eye on real experience. They don't get lost in abstractions, and the fruit of their reflections is always practical. He suggested that they tend to ask three questions:

> What are you talking about?
> Give me an example.
> So what?

In line with Macmurray's advice, we have tried to keep close to real experience by focusing on Matty Ventresca's life and death, and we have given numerous examples drawn from everyday life. But then, "So what?" What practical applications might these theological reflections have for us? Especially after taking apart some of our favorite myths, we should ask, "What positive ideas will keep our focus on living our lives in death's shadow?"

In this chapter, then, I will discuss five practical ways to keep death in our lives:

1. What to do with my inspirations
2. How to tell my story
3. How to tell *our* story
4. How to plan my death
5. How to do the will of God

WHAT TO DO WITH MY INSPIRATIONS

A 19th century Irishman by the name of William Burke possessed the remarkable gift of strangling people to death without leaving any bruises. They finally caught up with him and, despite his noble intentions of providing fresh bodies for dissection by medical researchers, executed him at Edinburgh in 1829. His sole legacy is a verb whose usefulness, unfortunately, far exceeds its use. To "burke" means to stifle without anyone noticing. To hush up. You would burke issues at work or burke the real story behind a relative's disappearance.

We also burke inspirations, both good and bad. On the one hand, we secretly choke off ideas when we realize they are going nowhere. Or we stifle the meaner impulses of our hearts to take revenge. On the other hand, we strangle kindly impulses toward others because they may interfere with our personal comfort.

Good people everywhere burke their bad ideas. This is what conscience does for a living; it buries, it suppresses. Unfortunately,

Pollyanna psychologists have given suppression a bad name, as if psychological health were simply a matter of letting every inner impulse go all the way. They seem to think that the human heart is beyond criticism, and therefore that people who are down on themselves just have to lighten up and everything will be fine.

But those who believe that good and evil are really different, who know how the heart constantly pulls in opposing directions, watch their hearts carefully. We might say that the heart is always in a *crisis*, a word that means "decision" in Greek. We stand between good and evil, with a choice. And this choice makes us practice suppression all the time. When we catch ourselves nursing lustful thoughts, more or less often we suppress them. When we rehearse the perfect squelch upon some arrogant acquaintance, we soon realize that these self-serving rehearsals are wrong, or at least that such a sweet triumph would never happen anyway, and we suppress the thought. When we get married we begin the work of dismantling the habit of looking around for a mate. When we have children, we let go of the serene pleasures of a quiet home. When we incur some ailment that requires inhalers, drops, shots or salves for the remainder of our lives, we die to the unencumbered life. Reminiscing about what we lost in this ongoing dying proves to be too painful; nostalgia ruins our determination to live well in our actual circumstances. In countless other ways, it should be obvious that suppression, drowning, burying, and dying are normal ways of living.

By realizing how often we die to our inspirations, we can better understand what the death at the end of our lives means. It is the asymptotic point toward which all these moral deaths head. It is the ultimate giving up of our entire persons after a lifetime of giving up one option after another. The common comparison we hear between physical death and moral death is not just metaphorical. These two deaths are intimately linked. The link lies not in what constitutes our physical life. Rather it lies at the level of what makes for a fully human life. Burking options is what makes our lives what they are. This core process of ongoing and ultimate self-sacrifice belongs to what is finest in us. A fully human life is not the life that doctors save; their focus is on keeping us breathing, digesting, seeing, hearing, walking. Rather, a fully human life lies on the stratum where we make decisions based on reason, something nothing else we know of does. It is the making of these decisions that requires that we throttle many of our inspirations.

Christians and some other religions have a way of symbolizing these moral deaths that helps us remember this is what life is all about. I am thinking of the ritual of baptism. It may come as a surprise to learn that in the New Testament, at least, baptism is not a symbol of purification. The authors did not mean to impress on us how God washes us clean of sin. The water is not soapy. To understand the Christian symbolism of baptism, it helps to realize that the people of the ancient Near East were terrified of water. God punished evildoers by the Flood. God swamped the Egyptians in the Red Sea. In the Mediterranean Sea swam the great beast, Leviathan. Storms on the Sea of Galilee rose quickly and swamped boats before they could reach shore. And remember the story about the disciple Peter walking across the water toward Jesus: when his faith sunk, so did he. It may seem odd to us that an experienced fisherman would panic here, but the story clearly means to convey the notion that unless Peter has faith, he will perish utterly in the menacing waters. Early Christian art portrays "the bark of Peter" as a fragile dinghy bobbing on a furious sea.

The point is that Christian baptism is a death by drowning. A Christian dies with nothing but faith in God and a hope that God will not let anyone who believes perish utterly. Simple as that. God will raise up Christ's disciples just as Christ was raised up. Christians whose ministers use baptism by immersion or perform baptisms during ordinary Sunday liturgies are fortunate. They benefit from a regular reminder that all of life is a baptism. Authentic living is all about drowning what is bad, rising to what is good, and trusting that even our physical deaths are consistent with the rule that "unless the seed fall to the ground and die, it shall not have life."

In an attempt to preserve this symbol of death by drowning, Catholic churches have traditionally put stoups of "holy water" inside their doorways. Their use is declining, however, and many are dry, probably because people forgot what the water means and, since Vatican II, were shrugging off meaningless rituals left and right. The original meaning of this water was to provide worshippers with a regular reminder of the baptism of Christ's death—a death they undergo every day.

Far from meaningless, this small reminder seems quite appropriate to represent the ongoing mystery of life-through-death in which we live. It would seem nourishing to the soul to gather a little of this water of death on our fingers and anoint our foreheads or hearts or draw a crucifix on our bodies. At that moment, we might say, "I die today with faith that God will give me life." That is, I die today to all the stupid and irresponsible ideas that will come to me. I die today to putting my own welfare above everyone else's. I die today to the urge to quit. I die today to the instinct to hoard. These all will I burke.

This brings us to the practical question: Which inspirations should I burke and which should I let breathe? Different religious and philosophical traditions give different instructions because inspirations are notoriously ambiguous. Take, for example, the teachings of various religions about the inspirations we call "desire." Some of the foremost representatives of Eastern religions regard human desires as an enemy to spiritual growth. Buddhism teaches that we should die to our attachment to desire, even to the persistent notion that we have a self. Hinduism teaches that we should turn away from the lure of success pulling on our consciousness. The Taoist teachings of Lao-Tsu took a similarly dim view of desires.

The great monotheistic scriptures—the Koran, the Torah and the New Testament—see the issue differently. They do not disparage all desire. Rather they see some desire as good and some as bad. It means dying to evil desires but fostering good desires. These moral deaths are not a blanket death to all desire; they are discriminating deaths. This follows from their beliefs in a personal God who has historical intentions. Because they regard God as a person with human qualities (as opposed to an unknowable, all-transcendent impersonal force), they project desires onto God. And if God has desires, then desires cannot be wrong in themselves. In contrast to the ahistorical perspectives of some strands of Buddhism, Hinduism, and Taoism, this is a God who *wants* something and who shares those desires with us. In Western religions, this discriminating view of desires has been supported not only by a long tradition of "discerning the spirits" but also by highly systematic reflections on ethics and the nature of desires. Eastern religions, on the other hand, rely on a less differentiated blending of practical advice and unsystematic speculations.

The New Testament often describes the heart as containing both good and evil desires: The parable of the weeds and wheat. Jesus' idea that what goes into your mouth counts nothing compared to what comes out of your heart. James' doctrine that disputes *between* people arise from cravings at war with each other *within* people. And the stories of the devil tempting Jesus as recorded by the synoptic evangelists.

One often overlooked reference to this battleground view of the heart occurs in Chapter 3 of the Letter to the Colossians—overlooked because it is badly translated. Most English language versions read "Let the peace of Christ *rule* in your hearts." Or some say *"reign* in your hearts." In these translations, the author seems to wish that the Colossians would experience their hearts being flooded with this peace like a land whose ruler keeps them permanently out of war. This is a nice sentiment, but it's not what the author meant. The word used for "rule" here is *brabeueto*, a term borrowed from sports. It means to rule like an umpire, not a king. That gives the sentence a refreshingly practical meaning. It is not a wish you might find on a Hallmark card. Rather it's a strategic instruction: "Let that peace that comes from Christ be the umpire in your heart by which you tell what's safe and what's out."

This one-liner corresponds well to later directives that Christians have inherited from hermits and philosophers of the 2nd, 3rd, and 4th centuries and from the mystics and reformers of the 16th. First, they assume that peace never completely rules the human heart; the heart is always a battleground of conflicting inspirations. They would consider today's quest for the permanently unanxious state, zealously pursued by serious psychologists no less than by committed substance abusers, as a living suicide. People who make inner calm their moral ideal tend to ignore the sound of that clanging bell of the spirit when trouble approaches. Deaf to the warning services of anxiety, they run headlong into problems and wind up with less peace than those who are accustomed to the struggle.

Second, these wise forbears analyzed how the two inner forces tend to work. Augustine proposed that the ultimate source of human evils is a *desire to dominate*. He considered that the fall of civilizations resulted essentially from people trying to lord it over others. Ignatius Loyola pointed out that the seemingly innocuous desires for money and fame were in reality the usual steps toward overweening pride. He recommended taking a pugnacious attitude against these innocent-looking desires by deliberate efforts to prefer poverty and humiliations in a loving imitation of Christ. He also noticed something that many other spiritual masters overlooked about desires. He taught that to identify good inspirations, one should listen not only to their content, but particularly to their *quality*, as measured by subjective feelings. And here we find an unexpected quirk in the way humans are equipped to make decisions.

Normally, to discern right from wrong, we let the mind take the lead. We analyze potential consequences, we apply traditional moral standards of what is fair or compassionate or honest, and we take into account any specific promises or obligations we may be under, including obligations to respect accepted teachings. But these criteria of the mind often fail us when it comes to sorting one "right" way from another, equally "right" way or, what is more common, when we have to decide between following an inspiration that seems good and just doing nothing.

The quirk is that here, in a person accustomed to doing what is right, letting the mind take the lead usually confuses the issue. Trying to pursue the most logical path often brings anxiety and frustration. Here it is better for the mind to hand the steering wheel over to the heart because a good person can trust feelings to assess and reject inspirations whose content is otherwise quite admirable. This is how discerning men and women discover their vocation. It is the clues in the heart, more than the mind, that are the voice of God calling them to a particular path in life. Lists of logical pros and cons never add up to a commitment. Even a long list of pros discovered by the mind can be outweighed by that one con, issuing from the heart, "It doesn't feel right."

Then, in persons who are more accustomed to compromising their consciences, the path to moral clarity is just the opposite. Following feelings only deepens their penchant for self-satisfaction, their pursuit of money and fame, and their urge to dominate others. What this person needs is the sting of the mind's reflection on the ultimate stupidity of their habits.

These two different ways of conducting our inner business of dying to certain alternatives make clear how feelings and thoughts usually work in the human psyche. Thoughts are "mental," while feelings are "commitmental." Thoughts show us what is logical, creative, intelligible, real. They bring a person to a plan, a realization, an acknowledgment. In contrast, feelings attach to what a person regards as valuable, worthwhile, good, wholesome. They move a person to action and personal commitment. They forgive hurts and error. Feelings are the glue that solidify a person's kind of dying, whether that dying is mortal or transforming. The rule seems to be that feelings tend to maintain a moral horizon (for good or ill) while thoughts tend to disrupt it. So, in people who hoard, their feelings spontaneously direct them to what will provide maximum comfort and self-satisfaction. But in people who suppress illogical, stupid, or silly inspirations, and who regularly put the good of the community above their own advantage, their feelings quickly direct them to the solution good for all.

Here is a capsule version of Ignatius' remarkable insight:

> A good person is prone to moral confusion by thinking too much; he or she should listen to the heart.

> A bad person is prone to moral decay by following the heart too much; he or she should listen to the mind.

For people going from good to better, Ignatius also provided an interesting thought experiment for identifying which of several good options may objectively be the best. In fact, it works well as an actual classroom experiment. Take a wet sponge and, holding it high over a rock on the floor, squeeze out some water. What happens to the water? It smashes and splashes. If an idea, even a "good" idea, enters consciousness like this, with agitation, spattering, and noise and rivulets running off in all directions, then one should be very careful before following up on it. Next, take the moist sponge and dip it into a pail of water. Now what happens to the water? It blends without noise. If the idea enters consciousness the way the water penetrates the sponge—quietly, invisibly, and fully—then one should prepare to put it into action. This exercise directs the heart to take the lead in decision-making. The heart's job is to weigh the *quality* of an inspiration as an indication of its objective value.

As Ignatius conceived it, this quiet, invisible, and full experience akin to water penetrating a moist sponge is a sign that the spirit of God is at work in consciousness. Notice that the final criterion by which we judge a thought worthwhile here is not the *content* of the thought (important though that be) but the *source* of the thought. Ignatius acted on the presumption that when God inspires a good person, the inspirations bring a lambent consolation at a deep level, even when the costs may be high in carrying it out. In the converse of this principle, if a good person thinks of some noble and charitable deed, but the thought enters consciousness like water falling on a rock, then the *source* of that is probably not God. Ignatius learned this lesson from his own experience. Under an inspiration to help others and to dedicate himself to God, he had fasted excessively and neglected his health. But this inspiration had come upon him with the same agitated *quality* that former inspirations to become a tough and respected knight had. Only later did he realize the danger of "good" inspirations that feel like water falling on a rock.

While this experiment is useful for beginners learning how to discern the movements of the heart, Ignatius usually gave much simpler advice about making a decision: "Lift the heart up to God." If I may speak from some modest experience, this is even easier for everyday living than the experimental test of seeing how water hits a rock and moves through a sponge. Lifting the heart to God simply means letting ourselves realize that God knows our hearts completely and, honoring the limits of what we know about a situation, that God wants to share with us the divine viewpoint on what is worthwhile here. We ask God, "What's really better here?" and very often, particularly in situations where our fears have gotten the better of us, it becomes clear what to do. It's as if we had our best friend beside us, a friend who has full knowledge of every detail in our situation and has a heart full of love for us. In what direction would our friend nod?

It should be evident by now that the dying that is necessary for real living requires that we let the love in our hearts take charge and let our minds follow suit. However, this spiritual work is not only for the sake of one person leading one good life. It is also part of the larger view of the scheme of things that keeps the entire human family in mind. It seems to be part of God's world-design that the progress of the human family will occur through people who let the divine eye for the good be their own. From a moral and historical perspective, the moral deaths necessary to liberate the minds and hearts of individuals also create the social structures that truly benefit people. It is these liberated hearts that assemble the cultural institutions capable of teaching citizens what to honor and preserve.

At the world's end, however it comes, the story of humanity will be a story of these *moral* deaths healing and creating the human family. The role of *mortal* deaths in the human story will have become sheerly preliminary because, in one way or another, all the ways we refused to follow out hearts will have been healed. We don't "practice" dying. The dying to bad inspirations that we do every day is actual dying, but an actual dying that gives all the meaning to our final dying. These are the dyings that, along with our bodies, God lifts up to eternal permanence and glory.

HOW TO TELL MY STORY

When we say that we "lead our lives," we leave the impression that we control all the turns our lives may take. A Frank Sinatra may boast, "I did it my way," as if his greatest accomplishment was to direct his life according to a script authored by himself. But in a much more profound sense "life leads us." Most of the challenges that will mark the turning points in our lives arise unexpectedly. If Sinatra "did it his way," all he did was prefer *his* way of responding to life, when often enough others had better ideas.

Life itself opens some opportunities and closes others. We don't easily notice these opportunities, however. Our psyches work in covert ways to focus our attention, so that besides the many choices we consciously face there are many others that we never saw. This covert work of the psyche is usually dominated by what we call "our story." If my story features me as a people-person, always ready to help others, then I will fail to notice my own needs to ask for help. If your story features you as an explorer, always seeking new experiences and new avenues of growth, then you will overlook the value of staying where you are and appreciating what you have.

Few people can recall making any deliberate choice about being a people-person, an explorer, or what-have-you, yet those subconscious choices fix our attention along restricted channels for our entire lives. It even seems that the majority of people take pride in the story they have embraced, which only justifies living with blinders. They assume that because they play the lead role in their personal stories, they must necessarily be the best interpreter of their experiences.

Now and then a strange character bursts onto our stage. Or the scenery falls over. Or there's no one in the audience. Or the orchestra plays the wrong song. That is, no matter what story we imagine ourselves living out, we often experience disruptions and are forced to act without preparation. A teacher who is a wizard to her high school math class is a shrinking violet at a mathematics convention. The otherwise insightful psychiatrist discovers too late that his children are neurotic messes. Then the mask must drop and the actor must deal from within.

Here is an important area where we must meet death—the deaths in our lives and the death at the end. We must face our mortality not with a script, not playing a role, not as a character, but with faith. But how can we carry on from one day to the next if we don't have some narrative framework for what we're about? Do we not need some dramatic pattern to give our lives meaning?

Let me illustrate this with someone's true story:

Carla was tired of bookkeeping. She'd been at it for a dozen years and was ready for something quite different. Her father had died recently, and her friends had always encouraged her to do something with her gift for telling stories. Unmarried, twenty-eight years old, she had the freedom to strike off in a new direction, but was unsure where to step first.

It is a familiar scene. A woman in the prime of her life realizing she needs to move on. Many have experienced this need to move on; some only wish they had the courage to try. It's a matter of becoming what one is supposed to be. It is a question of God's call, a vocation. It means finding the best identity offered to us by that particular intersection of spirit and history that made us who we are. It is an invitation to the light. Even though Carla is young, her unspoken awareness of the fact that someday her life will come to a finish beckons her to make something of the days she has.

There are, unfortunately, other voices that scold us for not becoming someone definite, someone clear, someone with an identity, which usually means someone with a title, a clear job description, and regular paychecks. So we have to fight against this love of clarity and security. We also have to be careful not to act out of sheer boredom. Sheer impatience for a sense of self can bend our ears to the barkers of excitement which deafen us to the quieter voices within that whisper good directions.

Jealousy is another such voice. We can feel resentment toward someone we wish we were. So we withhold small courtesies. Praise sticks in our throats. Then we feel disgust at ourselves. "How petty to resent another's good fortune, good looks, good friends! Surely I am bigger than that!" But the green-eyed demon fumes on. Self-esteem vanishes. We can hate the fact that we are ourselves. We know very well that the greener grass on the fence's other side is still grass; it will be no less dead than ours come winter. As our grievance festers, we lose our sense of God's invitation to become something beyond ourselves.

Or, besides boredom and jealousy, there's the insidious voice that says we are nothing. "Look at me. What have I ever done that counted for anything? Have I accomplished one worthwhile deed for anybody? If all the people whom I have helped sent me thank-you notes, I could count them on Captain Hook's right hand. And look at my face! The pores and wrinkles! This chin makes me look like an ostrich. People smile condescendingly at my condition. They're probably just tolerating me. They're waiting to see if I ever make anything of myself. So that's it. That's why I should strike off in a new direction. Become a somebody."

But who?

Carla heard the same voices. "I'll be a nun," she thought. "They look so happy, so neat in their outfits. They share life together. They take time to pray everyday. They really feel part of the church."

"No, I'll open a restaurant," she thought next, realizing the point is to *do* something, not just *be* something. "I'll serve simple but delicious food at good prices. People will love to come to 'Carla's Place.'" That thought lasted until about 3:00 o'clock when she considered the dirty dishes, the disgruntled employees, the unhappy customers, the city health codes, the late nights, and the long wait to be discovered by a food critic.

So, taking the advice of her friends, she began to think seriously about her storytelling talent. It was a great risk to step out relying on this odd talent. "If this doesn't work, it is really me that fails. It is all I have. It is who I am." She eventually landed a job telling stories on a local TV station. It was a small place, featuring a roster of evangelical preachers and ethnic programming. She felt comfortable among the Christians on the staff. They were not afraid to speak about God and prayer, and she appreciated that. On her own program, though, she avoided churchy talk and stuck to telling stories about ordinary people trying to accomplish ordinary things.

She had a particular knack for *not* drawing the moral conclusion with which her evangelical colleagues knocked people over the head. So her reputation grew. Things were clicking. She could tell a story about two squealing pigs and everyone would know she was blasting the mayor and police chief for fraud. She especially loved to parody the self-righteous religious types, the uppity, know-it-all, self-appointed saints. This is where her downfall began.

The TV evangelists who worked at her station became the target of her gentle but incisive allegories. She usually portrayed them as anal-retentive roosters, crowing and pecking, and driving everyone crazy with their over-alert intrusion into every business but their own. So they spoke to the management of the station. They circulated exaggerated stories about Carla's tolerance for abortion, her disrespect for religious authorities, her depiction of the station's potential advertisers as sharks eating all the little fish in the sea.

None of her enemies actually planned to kill her. They just wanted to silence her. They convinced the station owners to let her go. With thinly-veiled reasons and trumped-up charges, she was fired. But her determination remained, relying on the support she felt from many of her listeners. She decided to switch from TV to publishing. With the little income she had, she hired a staff and bought a printing operation with which to publish her parodies. Although her employees respected her and talked loyalty, some eventually connived with her enemies to impede her every move. It wasn't long before her print shop was fire-bombed.

"What am I doing?" she asked herself. "My so-called gift is my ruination! People like my stories, but nothing has really changed in this town. My employees seem faithful to my cause, but I'm not convinced they see the corruption I see. I doubt that they would carry on without me."

So the old self-doubt returned. She prayed she might learn why God brought her to this point. God was silent. The agony of failure only sharpened the point—the stabbing power—of her stories. Eventually the rage of her enemies ignited the fervor of justice in a sad young zealot with a gun. The end was easy. Tipped by an employee that she would be working late, he crept up to a window on her office and fired one bullet through her head.

Did she accomplish anything worthwhile? She died without an answer to that question. Neither she nor anyone else possessed any measure to assess whether her storytelling and writing were effective in reaching her goals. Although her death was violent, it is little different from ours when it comes to dying. We really don't know who we are or what we have been. We can line up our trophies on the mantle. Cover the staircase with pictures of our children and their children. Update the family album with pictures of picnics, the trip to Disneyland, the whopping good times with friends. These mirrors with which we surround ourselves are cloudy images of the reality of who we are. Notoriety is cheap, and recognitions of our service to institutions are always tempered by the realization that there are probably more plaques than people.

Identity is a strange thing. Everyone wants it but only those who forget about it have it. They do not "find" it; they cannot hold it; they will never frame it and hang it on the living room wall. It comes to them in the night and hovers over them in a way only other people can see. It can be bought only at the price of a certain ego blindness.

To be blunt, we cannot tell our story. We cannot live out our lives according to any script. We cannot consult our "identity" to see what fits and what doesn't. What is left is a kind of faith in ourselves, a faith only God can give, but a faith that believes, despite all evidence to the contrary, that we are worth something. This is a faith we need as death approaches, certainly. But we need it at every juncture in life where we feel dissatisfied with how we are doing. We need it when we get tired of our job. We need it when we wonder where our marriage is going. The truth is that God loves us. Or, to put it more forcefully, God dotes on us, God is enamored of us—God *likes* us.

We also need this faith when someone we love dies. Stories will be told, certainly. Accomplishments will be recited. But does anyone doubt that the worth of this person's life lies in decisions made in utmost secrecy, decisions destined for burial beyond the reach of all survivors—decisions to bite one's tongue, to suppress the unkind remark, to comfort the weary, to cover the naked, to visit those in whatever cell imprisons them? We need this faith to let our loved ones go up to God, who sees all these decisions and welcomes our friend with perfect knowledge of who he or she really is.

We particularly need to have this faith regarding those of whom we are jealous. The best of them care nothing about their identity, in which case we do well to honor their integrity. The rest care so much about their identify that they fabricate a Potemkin village of their face to show everyone how fine they're doing, in which case we can remind ourselves that their real worth, though completely hidden, is there nonetheless.

The story of Carla is true. For purposes of insight, I changed her name and gender and added little extra detail. Her real name is Jesus, the man, the storyteller, the one with a vision, the one betrayed, the one who did not know what to do next because he could see clearly what God was up to. This is the one whose followers believe God raised up, to whom was given the name above every other name.

His failure to become what he wanted to be is God's way of telling everyone, "The Lord is very near. There is no need to worry." This is the same assurance Krisha gives Arjuna, as recorded in the final chapter of the *Bhagavad Gita:* "Center your mind on me, and you will come to me. I promise you truly, you are dear to me. Come to me alone and I shall free you from all sins. You need not grieve."

Here is where many who seek God turn away. When they realize that loving God all the way does not make their lives any easier, when they discover to their dismay that the light of a deeper faith also darkens the shadows, then they entertain second thoughts about this quiet wish for ultimates. What is at stake is not mere comfort or money. They stand poised to lay down life's big chips: their personal sense of fulfillment, that feeling of self-satisfaction over a job well done. If they let that go, how will they know how to live? Losing their familiar measuring stick for what is worthwhile, they are panic-struck at the thought of trusting in God's spirit within—not as a permanent possession but as an ongoing free gift.

Loving God demands an ever deepening and frightening faith. It is ever deepening because with each act of faith in God, we let fall another human crutch until we can hardly believe how we can remain standing. This is what happens to everyone who lets God be their God. Likewise it demands an ever deepening hope—one that hopes more in the presence of spiritual power at life's unpredictable junctures than in "hopes" for outcomes we think would be best.

Christians tend to think God was somehow obligated to raise Jesus from the dead because, after all, this was God's "son." An overemphasis on this doctrine overshadowed the reality that Jesus of Nazareth was a free person, free to make a genuine decision when tempted to do evil. As a result, many believers in Jesus forget that God is ultimately, essentially, and absolutely free. They easily think that any kind of redemption from the terrors of death that God has arranged is something necessitated by some privileged "nature" of Jesus rather than a free gift.

But if we look at it all from Jesus' point of view—which our story of Carla has attempted to convey—we feel no assurance at all that God is obligated to do anything on our behalf. Jesus had no New Testament to read for guidance any more than Carla had an outline to follow. Many religions portray God as loving and kind. What many of them overlook (and indeed many Christians overlook) is that God is also *free*. All of us, of whatever religion, go to our deaths like Jesus did—scared of God's terrifying freedom to ignore everything about us, yet loving God with a hope that does not want to quit.

HOW TO TELL *OUR* STORY

If I cannot tell my story but rather have to live it out, the same goes for "our" story—the symbols and myths about our family, culture, religious groups, or friends that give our communities an identity. Just think of the many variations on doctrines of "manifest destiny" that citizens were taught in order to justify taking over a neighboring country. Even oppressed groups are tempted to cry "victim!" at every political change that is not to their advantage. Stories like these can be dangerous rationalizations for greed as well as deliberately misleading excuses for deficiencies. Still, it is difficult not to create a national or cultural story. Each generation tells its own story as present experience becomes history. It is important to fashion a narrative about who we are in order to educate our children about where they are from.

So we need to discern between stories. To do that, it helps to notice that we have a choice between two kinds of stories, which we can illustrate by an example taken from American patriotism.

D-Day, in 1944, saw the invasion of France by the Allies and the beginning of the end of the Second World War. It was a day in which thousands of soldiers laid down their lives for their fellow citizens. We who enjoy democracy live out our lives in an unpayable debt to them—young men, for the most part, to whom the machinations of governments assigned the role of national martyr.

Part of us wants to fashion a simple vignette out a terrible day. We want to remember brave soldiers charging into battle and turning the tide of a war waged by a madman. These men were justifiably afraid; many died and many more were permanently maimed. But we like to think of the survivors as holding their heads high with honorable pride over what was a courageous act. It is important to keep this simplified view alive: It helps us remember sacrifices we should be ashamed to forget.

But while preserving national memory is important, so too is historical accuracy. Finding out what really went on, behind the scenes, as it were, far better reveals the devisings of human hearts. Interviews with combatants and field strategists give us a better glimpse of the awful reality of that war. Most survivors deny feeling anything like courage; they report that they simply tried to stay alive. General Eisenhower seems to have preferred that the least experienced soldiers be selected for D-Day because he feared that veterans, with their knowledge of horror, might revolt. So, cheering each other on, showing a brave face to hide a terrified mind, these callow young men plunged into battle.

A German veteran interviewed on the radio said that he and all his comrades in arms knew that the Allies would win. Half the "cannons" sticking out of pill boxes were telephone poles, placed there to fool the Allied reconnaissance photographers flying overhead. German soldiers were lads pulled from high school, handed a gun that often misfired, and shoved up to the front line. But, owing to myopic ambition among the German leadership, the lost war had not yet lost sufficient lives to be "over."

Stories of the American Civil War fall similarly into two types. Either they are simple vignettes of courage conquering evil or else deeply complex tales of posturing generals and boys shooting each other for uncertain gain.

The vignettes are by far the more dangerous stories. True, they educate the young in national pride. They help us remember the ultimate sacrifices made by others on our behalf. They remind us of the unfairness by which we are alive because others are not. But these vignettes are more dangerous than historical accounts because they depict history as essentially as a kind of gang warfare. Us against them. Worse, they typically claim that God is "on our side." They never raise the possibility that "our" cause may have been immoral. By assuming that history means taking sides, they expect that good and bad are distributed accordingly. Once a nation deems another as "bad," then soldiers feel a justification to attack its people and plunder their belongings.

Historiography, the study of history with a view to telling what really happened, is a relative newcomer to the human sciences—but a welcomed arrival. It contributes far more to the welfare of humankind than the historical myths. Certainly there are complex problems that come with trying to explain the causes and trends in historical events, but at least historiographers try to explain and to evaluate with some objectivity. They do not aim to promote one side above another. As a result, they convey a much more accurate picture of the unfolding of human history. What is more, they teach lessons to a citizenry that are more important than national pride. For example, they have the power to show how terrible the effects of arrogance can be in a single, ambitious leader. They can impress on the young how stupid it is to nourish ethnic hatred. They can convince educators how important it is to pursue complete explanations rather than settle for superficial views of the goings on of a people.

One lesson in particular we should not overlook. Great historical disasters result not only from the *actions of evil* people; they result as much from the *failures of good* people to act. No doubt, it required tremendous courage for individuals to actively resist the war machine assembled by Nazi Germany, and most Germans, Austrians, Hungarians, Jews, Gypsies, ministers, priests, homosexuals or scholars who resisted, laid down their lives for their friends. And among that majority of people who did not take such active stands, most simply had little idea of what was going on or, if they did, had no assurance that speaking out would do any good. So we should not easily condemn those individuals who failed to put their necks on the block for no clear purpose.

What remains a great historical scandal, however, is the silence of practically every organized religion over the known Nazi and Russian policies of ethnic purgings. Although it was only later that the general public became aware of the horrendous pogroms toward which they were headed, the underlying ideas and policies were public knowledge for years. Many religious leaders kept silent to protect the lives of their congregations. This shows admirable care on one level, but this rationale also raises questions about life and death that must be faced: Does the duty to prevent death in one's community override the duty to prevent death elsewhere? Is it really better for a religious community to survive in silence than to perish speaking up for others? In other words, is it better that *they* die than *we* die?

The religions we are talking about here are mainly Christian. In Germany, Jewish leaders represented the victims, and many resisted to the point of martyrdom. Many others cried out, through channels both secret and overt, to a world that could not believe its ears. Not only did few outsiders respond to Jewish cries for help, fewer still understood the *theological* issue for Jews here. God's mandate to the Jews has always been "to live." The vocation of the Jew lies in living this life, not preparing for an afterlife. It lies in living in a community in history, not as an isolated individual. So the Nazi threat challenged every Jew not merely on the level of ordinary self-preservation but, most significantly, on the level of obedience to God's will.

For Christians, this has raised two questions. The first is how Christianity dispossessed itself of this Jewish inheritance that regarded the vocation to increase and multiply as the primeval meaning to obeying the will of God. Many people interpreted the Christian doctrine of the resurrection as a change in vocation from a this-worldly living together to a next-worldly individual salvation. That unfortunate development would take a few history books to explain, but to my mind the development was not entirely good for Christianity.

The second question it raises is an equally difficult theological issue and more pertinent to our discussion of the meaning of life-unto-death in Christian doctrine. We can pose it as follows: Should the ancient Christian doctrine of imitating Christ be a standard of behavior not only for individuals but for groups as well? Jesus allowed his life to be cut short rather than keep quiet. Should the same be true of a community that looks to Christ as its model? That is, does the example of Jesus, the individual, extend to an entire group? Should a community prefer to die rather than be quiet in the face of evil? In particular, should the Vatican have endangered the lives of Catholics throughout Germany by protesting against Nazi policies of exterminating Jews and the handicapped? Should Dietrich Bonhoeffer have challenged his Evangelical congregation to speak out? It is difficult to believe that no Christian leaders entertained any thought of protesting these outrages. And even today, religious leaders condemn that scandalous silence only in the meekest of language.

This problem is not restricted to Christians. As we have seen, practically all religions and philosophies preach self-sacrifice, self-denial, self-death. But only to individuals. As far as I know, no one has been able to translate this moral death in terms applicable to community.

At least we know that an entire religious group, as a community of belief and practice, has obligations to other groups. As groups recall how they closed their hearts when God provided the inspirations, we may hope that they feel shame, not self-justification. But we may also hope that our religious leaders today take seriously the ancient and revered doctrine that we have discussed here from many angles, namely, that God created us as a community in history first; our individuality springs from that and ultimately contributes to that, and not vice-versa. Since these leaders have obligations to lead the community forward, not simply give advice to individuals on the virtuous life, they need to take hard looks at the sin of community silence.

Concerning D-Day, we ought to accept that any blame for this terrible sacrifice of innocent lives—on both sides—should include blame for the sin of silence. It is a pious and undeserved luxury to blame Hitler and let it go at that. The horror of that war resulted from the millions of sins of omission and only a few sins of commission. People looking for God in D-Day will find divinity first in their personal experience of, on one side of their hearts, divine inspirations to speak and, on the other, their human compulsion to lie low. This is the kind of sin that, taken collectively, supports the rise of mad dictators and their heartless ravaging of these, our brothers and sisters. This is an awful and yet a common sin we share with one another.

If this is what D-Day tells us about the moral life, then it also tells us something about how God means to guide history. The fact that a multitude of sins of omission are necessary for any single sin of commission to ruin things says that when God speaks in our hearts, it is very seldom in *don't*'s. God speaks most often in *do*'s. Just as evil enters the hearts of individuals where they fail to denounce this alien intruder, so the evil of individuals spreads through communities that fail to condemn it. Had a few dozen religious or national communities had risked their security by speaking out in the late 30s against the racist ideals of the Nazi party, millions upon millions of people may have lived to see life's natural end. This is 20/20 hindsight, of course, but there is a valuable lesson for *communities* who professes belief in a God who cares: Silence can be a community's mortal sin.

It looks like God's strategy for sharing life with us is through inspirations to blow the whistle on wrongdoing. These inspirations are particularly important in leaders of a community. Their role is not merely to maintain the unity of the community; at times it is to lead that community to be a witness to the truth. The risks to one's security and reputation may be high, and even higher are the risks to the security of one's community, but are these not the very *deaths* by which God redeems situations?

HOW TO PLAN MY DEATH

Our fourth practical advice on how to live in death's shadow deals directly with our physical deaths. TV documentaries on funeral rites show us a wide diversity in the ways people have dealt with death over the centuries. But, beginning only a quarter of a century ago, a new question has come up about how we die. We currently are undergoing a profound shift in how we experience living in the shadow of death. We now experience an unprecedented emergence of opportunities to choose the manner in which we die. And this new condition of the human spirit raises new questions about how we make life-and-death decisions.

I am speaking about the fact that more people "manage" their deaths today than ever before in history. That is, the dying person has taken steps to control how quickly death comes and whether by an unpreventable illness or by a newly available set of self-imposed deaths often described as "passive suicide." These attempts to play a more active role in how one dies have been motived in part by tales of fateful decisions to "pull the plug" and the ensuing guilt borne by survivors. In the United States, they have also been motivated by recent changes in federal law.

It wasn't very long ago that the ethics of withdrawing artificial life support centered exclusively around someone in a coma, and not many of us worried about that. Gradually, however, the focus of attention has shifted from concern over the somewhat remote possibility of a vegetative life to the far more likely possibility that one's memory may vanish while everything else functions adequately. The likelihood of the normal adult spending his or her last years with dementia has grown to frightening proportions. Currently, almost half the people over eighty-four suffer from some form of dementia. This percentage will increase as more people improve their health habits and, on the average, live longer. To date, there is no evidence that research in dementia-preventing technology will decrease this percentage in the near future.

Perhaps the reason we associate dementia in the elderly so closely with death is that, for them, dementia *is* a death—a death of memories, memories that form their most precious sediment after their friends die and their children move them to a retirement home. They lose short-term recollection. They forget what day it is. They blank on their children's names. While they may feel as though they are thinking, they have lost touch with the reserve of words with which to share their thoughts. They start a sentence, pause to grope for a word, and then forget what they started to say.

Many experts in elder-care separate dementia from dying. They stress that dementia not a terminal illness. It is a disease and should be treated as such. That is, we should not abandon the confused person simply because this condition is "normal" for someone that age. The demented often retain a sense of creativity, surprise, and curiosity. We can help keep these spiritual faculties going by poring over old photographs or reading the newspaper together. The demented also commonly suffer from depression, which in most cases can and should be treated with drugs.

Still, when dementia is extreme and is combined with a loss of motor skills, it raises the possibility that we can make a choice between dying of starvation or living as a semi-vegetable. The elderly in whom dementia is beginning, or who anticipate it, contemplate the day when they can no longer decide rationally for themselves. They don't want to die mentally and go on physically.

Anticipating dementia, many people now give explicit directions not to be put on artificial life support. "Don't put me on any machines!" Grandma said. In the United States, the Patient Self-Determination Act of 1991 required hospitals to inform patients of the availability of a "living will" and the appointment of a "durable power of attorney." Grandma now has the means of making her wishes known effectively.

Current laws and customs, buttressed by a long-standing moral principle that drew a line at "extraordinary means," honor such advance directives about high-tech and expensive life support systems.

We are getting used to the idea that we do not have to spend all our savings on space-age equipment that does little more than keep us breathing.

While many people seem comfortable with the idea that they should not be put on a ventilator if attempts to maintain their lives are futile, many more hesitate to forgo antibiotics, food, and water. Intravenous feeding is a simple procedure, and antibiotics are cheap and effective, so we naturally resist the idea of withholding them from a person nearing death. That is, why in the world would we let someone die when keeping them alive is so easy? This has raised a question in a way that was unheard of thirty years ago. Should I decide under what conditions I clearly would *not* want intravenous feeding and medicine? If I imagine a future in which I cannot recognize anyone I love, I cannot think intelligently, I cannot tell the difference between what's going on around me and my own daydreams, and if, on top of all of this, I cannot feed myself and can be spoon-fed only with great difficulty because I've lost my appetite, then I face a difficult decision: Shall I tell my loved ones now, while I have my faculties, that I would choose to die by starvation under these circumstances? Shall I tell them now that I don't want antibiotics if I reach that awful state? It is a choice our grandparents never faced.

Some say it is even more difficult when you have to decide for someone else. Suppose you are the proxy for someone incapable of deciding—for example, a brain-damaged child or an irreversibly demented parent. Where we might easily give directives for ourselves that we want to forgo artificial life support in certain conditions of extremity, it appears more difficult to make this decision for someone else who is already incapacitated. On the one hand, any proxy will feel the pressure of responsibility for a helpless person's death, and perhaps feel guilty even *thinking* about the fact that an inheritance would better go into their bank accounts rather than to hospitals or nursing homes. On the other, a proxy will anticipate relief from a longstanding emotional and financial burden on the family, as well as a genuine desire that a loved one suffer no further pain.

Here, medical ethics usually follows the rule of patient autonomy. That is, the rule for telling the doctor what to do is to follow the principle of honoring patient self-determination first. You represent, as best you can, what the demented person probably wants. This means that, as a proxy, you do *not* do what *you* think is best. You state what the patient prefers. Rather than "making the decision" for someone else, a proxy's duty is to "convey the decision" of someone else.

Imagine a grown daughter acting as proxy for her comatose father. Her obligation is simply to determine what *his wishes* might be. She is not making a decision; she is stating a judgment of fact as far as she can ascertain it. A strict adherence to this rule actually eases the moral burden of most proxy interventions. Even where a terminally ill father left no written directives, his spouse or children usually know what he would want. Medical and pastoral personnel in hospitals and nursing homes need to inform the proxies and families of the dying person about this limit to their responsibility to help lift the false burden of having to make a terrible decision.

If, then, the proxy's responsibility is to represent the dying person's choice, each of us, as a person who will die, faces a decision about how we want that death to happen. Shall I choose, if I lose all memory and be unable to feed myself, to forgo antibiotics and any form of nutrition and hydration, whether intravenous or spoon-feeding? Whether or not I leave written instructions, whether or not I just casually mention my wishes to my family, this is a decision I ought to make. If I don't, if I keep postponing the issue, the odds are fairly high that I will be unable to make the decision. In that situation, because medicine defaults to keeping me alive, I may impose a burden on my loved ones that I never intended.

Some will ask, Do I have any *right* to refuse life-sustaining means that can no longer be considered extraordinary? That is, am I *justified* in refusing ordinary food, water, and antibiotics? There are two problems with this objection. One, it interprets "extraordinary" as meaning *technical* and *expensive*. However, the "extraordinary means" criterion as taught in traditional ethics means *extraordinarily high loss for too little benefit*. It is an alternative way of stating the long-accepted ethical principle of proportionality applied to end-of-life conditions. Thus, in cases of persistent vegetative states, the "extraordinary means" principle recognizes that even very cheap life-sustaining devices may be too high a price to pay for the "benefit" of lengthening a life with extremely poor quality. The "price" is not the dollar cost of medical procedures but the lengthening of a person's agony.

The other problem with asking whether I have a right to refuse life-sustaining procedures is that a Yes answer is never really helpful. Having the right to refuse treatment tells me nothing about whether I should. For example, most people would agree that we have a right to refuse to donate blood, but this doesn't make such refusals always good. Human rights are basically defensive. They aim to prevent external interference with the exercise of our freedom to live authentic lives. But rights do not tell us how to act authentically. "Free" countries boast freedom of speech, but this does not provide guidance in what to say. They boast freedom of association, but give no directives on what kinds of association benefit anyone's human condition. So, having a right to forgo any form of life support really means simply that we are free to make a choice, nothing more.

It is not an easy question to answer. Socrates, swirling the hemlock in his cup, posed the question of how he should die: "Which is better here? Life or death? Only the gods know." I doubt that we will ever answer that question in a general way. I cannot think of any common principles about dying from which each person can logically deduce that he or she should die. Each person is entirely unique and self-determining. How I will die is a matter of committing myself, not making a deduction. Even after we have exhausted all available guidance from our tradition and our friends, we still must make a determination about our persons. We still must take responsibility, and that means doing something entirely new.

Choosing the pace and conditions of our death means putting our autograph on a decision. There is not even much guidance in ancient religious texts. The question of managing our deaths had not occurred to anyone because ancient medicine did not prolong dying as it does today. The patient either got better or just died. Today, individuals must answer it for themselves as they weigh their real alternatives.

It must be said, of course, that most of us have loved ones to consult. Indeed, the emphasis on patient autonomy that has held center stage among medical doctors for several decades is now yielding place to a more communitarian principle. While we all live in an existential solitude to a certain extent, that doesn't mean we live alone. In most of our major life decisions, we consult those who know us and care for us. We even imagine what dead parents would advise. It is difficult to imagine that those who have made difficult decisions in utter solitude would claim that they were uninfluenced by any other person.

More than ever before in history, we can make choices about the manner of death we prefer, whether or not fate robs us of the outcome we desire. It is in facing these choices that we must look at the extent to which we rely on others. In so doing, we make a fundamental option to be a particular kind of person. At one extreme is the self-contained person who gathers data and, in an utterly solitary decision, chooses a manner of death. At the opposite extreme is the totally dependent person who relies on the suggestions, hopes, and expectations of others without a thought given to personal responsibility. In the grand experiment that human history is, most people seek a middle ground where the decision is neither autonomous nor received but rather is reached together, with all parties feeling responsible for it.

Most people will trust the "sense of the common" here. The human thing to do is to reach consensus with our loved ones about our manner of dying—neither withdrawing into a romanticized existential solitude nor begging those we respect to tell us what to do. A 100 percent consensus is not always possible, of course, but talking about it with others helps to put things into perspective.

For my part, if I reach an irreversible condition where I cannot recognize anyone I love, and I lose my sense of humor, and if I can no longer feed myself—or don't want to feed myself—then, please, let me die. Let me yield to nature's course as the absence of food and water breaks down my metabolism. A "dry" death like this, health care professionals tell us, is far less painful than a "wet" death. The loss of appetite is the dying body's natural process. I take this stand because I watched my parents die of cancer while we kept on feeding them. I heard their death rattles and watched their agony, an agony that I now realize was preventable. But I do not want to take this stand about my death alone. I hope to listen to my wife, family, and friends too. I hope to keep in mind—whatever mind I may have—that they are walking into this death with me. I want to respect their opinion.

Am I managing my own death? Of course I am. Is there something wrong with this? I don't think so. These death-managing decisions reinforce the poignant metaphor we have been using for the decisions we make every day about "moral" deaths. Men and women have been managing how they "die" in a moral sense ever since Adam and Eve. So if the real meaning of physical death is rooted in moral deaths, then manage we must.

HOW TO DO THE WILL OF GOD

These recently-emerging opportunities to make choices about our physical deaths are not really something new to the *manner* in which we should make our choices. We still rely on conscience and intelligence. That conscience and intelligence may be our own when we face a choice which our tradition has not sufficiently come to terms with. Or it may be the conscience and intelligence of our forebears. These choices became tested and established as "tradition" by those who came after them, but both their originating choices and their subsequent testing were always a matter of conscience and intelligence.

This conclusion goes down hard in people who believe that God writes books and whispers messages into the ears of prophets. Some go so far as to teach that conscience and intelligence are the causes of people forgetting God. They warn us, "You can't just follow your own conscience—you have to obey God!" And they preach, "God's ways are not our ways." They will recommend that people forget human wonder. They will downplay painstaking reflection and promote instead some book or guru that has all the answers. Their injunction against thinking has to be absolute, however. Once wonder about history gets any foothold in consciousness, once people decide to find answers to relevant questions rather than suppress them, there is nothing to prevent them from wondering how God's will exercises dominion over human affairs.

Still, the decision to set conditions on how one will die is so deeply personal that even after one has acknowledged the priority of conscience, actually making that decision is ethically frightening. After all, unlike other moral risks, you cannot look back on the death you arranged for yourself and do better next time. To state in a "living will" that under certain circumstances, you prefer to forgo food and water is asking for a heavy moral burden. Although logical reasoning about "rights to die" and "duties to live" is valuable, logic is cold comfort for hard decisions.

Maybe we can ease that ethical and existential panic somewhat by asking how our choices about dying can be "God's will." Perhaps we can give some explanation to those hesitant to trump the word of authorities with the word of conscience if we consider how such a personal choice can possibly be God's work. This lifts the question a level above the realm of ethical reasoning and considers it within the realm of a personal relationship with God. This seems the more ordinary and more appropriate way to frame the question because it uses terms that are familiar to most people, namely, "Does God want this?"

Technological and economic changes have always raised new moral questions throughout history. These are questions people had to face without the clear guidance of principles developed by their traditions. Even our revered spiritual ancestors did not always see clearly what God may have wanted; it usually took later tradition to sort that out and, once it did, past practices appear shocking in their moral naiveté. Our past is strewn with examples. Hebrews took retribution on those who wronged them, they killed not only the offenders but their entire families as well. The first generation of Christians had no clear word from Jesus whether Gentiles could be considered equal to Jews in the eyes of God. In the Middle Ages, popes considered the burning of witches an act of piety and the castrating of Vienna choirboys an act of divine praise. Only in the last two hundred years have we seriously considered that slavery might be wrong, and in the last fifty years realized that women might be fully the equal of men. Anyone claiming that all these people failed to carry out God's will overlooks the simple fact that they didn't *know* that these policies were immoral. Human knowledge about morality is evolving, and rather slowly.

So how does God reveal the divine will? How do divine values end up in human hearts and direct human history? It seems that, rather than intervene in history by sending directives from above, God prefers that we take responsibility for what our consciences suggest. Certainly, we count on our traditions, laws, and historical examples for guidance. Of course, many will pray to God for direction. Some may experience a divine inspiration about what the divine will may be (leaving them with the problem of how to convince everyone else). But by far the most common experience is that God does not give much conviction, despite our petitions. Even such seemingly unequivocal divine mandates as "Thou Shalt Not Kill" give meagre comfort to a family that decides to leave their comatose mother on a ventilator for years.

We cannot accuse God of silence, however. God has been responsible for the traditions we inherited, the exemplars we admire, the sacred writings, and the teachings of our religions. God has also been responsible for the inspirations in our hearts by which we select among the traditions and examplars around us. But God has left us free. It is up to us to put together the beckonings from our historical situations and the penchants of our hearts. It is up to us to make sense of the different ways God speaks.

Still, even though God is not silent, neither does God give information. We must consider seriously that as each new moral problem appears in history, God brings forth good through human moral risk. That is, when we do what we think is best, even though we fall short of certitude, and even should hindsight later prove us wrong, God is still at work. Does this view diminish God's dominion? Does it depict a God who is helpless to prevent evil and error in the world? Not if we take seriously the belief that God shares divine life with us in the struggle to be fully human. The great religions of the world vary somewhat on this belief, but all of them entertain it to some extent. The belief implies that we are already in union with God in our searching. God is not waiting to see if we pick the correct path that leads us deeper into divine life; the uncertain choice itself, made with the purpose of doing what is right, is already a deeper share in God's inner life.

I have found it helpful to distinguish three kinds of moral resolution: moral *certitude*, moral *conviction*, and moral *assurance*. They are all states of mind, but they stand on very different grounds of resolve. Moral *certitude* comes when neither we nor anyone else has any question about the issue. We have moral certitude that killing someone for the sheer feeling of power is wrong. No one doubts this. Moral *conviction* comes when we take a stand against the opinion of some others. People who speak on the morality of abortion are convinced of their position, but as long as other decent people disagree, they may be prepared to die for their *conviction*, but they cannot claim to have the same kind of resolve that amounts to *certitude*. Finally, moral *assurance* comes when we rely on the love of others to support us when our moral convictions are hesitant. Assurance comes with faith in love, not faith in our reasoning powers. Assurance adds to conviction the possibility that we may be wrong but that if we are, our friends will help us draw good from our error. Such moral assurance is not only a gift from friends around us. It is also an invitation of the divine within us, to the degree that our love is the doing of God.

Of the three kinds of moral resolution, moral certitude is the most dangerous. There are some who claim to be able to discern the will of God in specific matters in a way that brings them certitude. It would be a comfort if there were such a scheme. God-loving individuals would enjoy an unassailable certainty about which path to take, which option to choose. However, as soon as the principle became accepted that some select people could know the will of God, the gates to the power-hungry would swing wide open. We have seen this in the insular, gnostic groups living in total submission to some self-proclaimed master who holds the golden key to the thoughts of God. We see it too in the piously vested leaders of many high churches. To them, life is a game—not in the sense that it is trivial, but that it has rules dictating the correctness of all possible moves. We cannot reach home base unless we take the right steps at every roll of the dice, and one of the steps is to listen to religious leaders.

Moral conviction is the more honest, more human stance. Despite unresolved questions, we have to take a stand. We cannot stand on evidence and analysis alone, since others analyze evidence differently. We stand also on values that we cannot completely articulate, values that we have inherited and values that we have come to on our own. And we stand on a willingness to stick with our position. That is, the very fact that we make a commitment says we believe enough in our own resources to follow a given path no matter where it leads. Moral conviction, however, still needs some sense of hope, of trust that taking a stand, even if wrong, is better than taking no stand at all.

That sense of trust is moral assurance. Moral assurance is the assurance from those who love us that all shall be well. All manner of things shall be well. For those who believe in a loving God, moral assurance is the belief that our future failures will be forgiven, that we are not doomed to shame, despite the shameful things we do. True, God prefers that we "work out our salvation in fear and trembling." True, God prefers that we take responsibility upon our shoulders. True, we should resist the notion that anyone can have certitude about the divine will. True, therefore, that we have only our faith to rely on. But our faith is not a mere hope that God will forgive our mistakes. Rather it is a faith that at each step of the way God inspires anyone who asks for inspiration. This faith affirms not only that God will be faithful to each of us but that God will be faithful to the human community as it evolves through history. Provided that we are open to mutual forgiveness and to the humble admission that past moral standards may have been in error, God will be faithful to our communities and lead us to carry out the divine will—a will revealed not through religious channels that bring certitude, but rather through affective channels that bring conviction through assurance. It is up to us to allow the forces of assurance to support our convictions.

In many different ways, I have been stressing how God reveals divine values to us mainly to nourish the growth of the human family. I should remind readers that these divine values are quite familiar. For example: It is better to return good for evil; it is better to suffer evil than to inflict it; it is better to die than to compromise your conscience; it is better to make decisions based on objective worth rather than on subjective payoff. God seems to will these not simply for our personal virtue, and not simply to help us get along together, but, in addition, that the entire human family will improve over time. The human vocation, the divine invitation, seems to be that we love not only each other, but that we take with utmost seriousness our obligation to love the generations of our human family yet to come.

What does this mean, then, for the new and difficult question about managing death that we face as we move into the third millennium? When our spirits collapse beyond a certain point, is it better for the human family that we refuse ordinary life-sustaining treatment? Or is it better that we accept it? The courageous moral risks taken by individuals are not private; they also contribute to the store of real examples that a community draws upon to illustrate what it believes is right and wrong.

"Religious tradition" in its most essential and most revered sense, is the passing on of hard-won wisdom. We have yet to win that wisdom with regard to managing our deaths. So today, we are taking part in the birth of what we hope will be an honored tradition. When you or I sit down to fill out a "living will" or an "advance directives" document, the struggles of our conscience represent not merely our own salvation. They represent the Spirit of God moving history forward a little. The ethical discomfort we feel is an experience of God's own life filling our souls for the sake of souls connected up and down history. The theological comfort we may feel is knowing that this is true no matter what we write there.

How, then, do we do the will of God? With uncertain minds and assured hearts. Certitude about God's will is mostly unavailable, and even where we have it, it resulted from the moral risks of our spiritual ancestors who lacked it. We *do* the will of God by doing works we believe are good, with faith that God and the good neighbor will provide the appropriate doses of forgiveness and inspiration.

CHAPTER 7
Meeting Death with Faith

Though never over, time is up,
Time for names, account for all that passed.
So let the light befall on all,
Find more answers then than could be asked.

Like geologists examining a glacier, we have examined the mystery of death from many sides. We still cannot see the whole of it. But just as geologists rely on color photography, video taping, infra-red photos, satellite scans, ultrasound probes, and magnetic indicators, so we use different kinds of "film" to record our impressions—a narrative of a real boy's death, traditional myths and modern symbolic language, insight into processes, rich metaphors, lean dogmas, complex hermeneutics, bold propositions about history, reflections on how reflection itself works in these different modes, and the bare affirmations of faith. As the geologists take care to observe the limits of each kind of recording device, we also noted the limits of each kind of our records lest we interpret any one of them beyond what it can convey.

So, for example, our symbolic narratives about Creation are meant to make an affirmation about our origins and destiny, but they do not provide a philosophic razor for slicing away descriptions of *how* the race began and how it will end. Our symbols work to combine images and feelings in the mind, so that we can carry a consistent attitude toward dying, but they do not provide a conceptualized explanation about it. Meditation and analysis give us ideas about the workings of death— whether physical or moral and, if moral, whether "mortal" or "transforming"—but these distinctions may be replaced by better categories that better explain the kinds of death we die. Contemplation and dogma aim to uncover the truth by giving us the bare bones of affirmations and negations. They do not explain nor, by themselves, make belief heartfelt, yet without them the heart would have nothing to feel.

THE SHARED QUESTION

Behind these various approaches, there is one factor that links us together: we are fascinated about death but wish it on no one. Matty's death remains tragic despite the fact that the short life he enjoyed was flooded with sunshine. Death beckons us yet threatens us. Because we both fear it and wonder about it, we have had to walk a narrow path between obsession and denial, between taking death to be the ultimate enemy and living as though we would never die. In this mélange of curiosity and dread, it is no wonder that the human race has churned out so many explanations about the meaning of death and how we should live before that day. But here is where we meet each other as we are, here is where we share a common question, even though we may diverge as we each formulate our answers.

In that dark nexus of the shared question, there also seems to be one answer that those who believe in God hold in common, one truth they share, one rock on which they stand and to which they return when they lose their way. They believe that death is God's idea for loving us. Perhaps death entered the world because of sin, as the Hebrew and Christian scriptures say. Or perhaps death was part of the divine plan from the beginning, as taught in Islam. In any case, death is an irrevocable part of our experience of life and, rather than an obstacle to God's kind purposes and more than just a means to an end, we believe that death is a stamp of God's self-giving essence.

We cannot prove this. It is a matter of faith, of trust in God, of a belief we cannot call certitude. Yet the idea that death may be necessary for humans to find fulfillment in God has occurred to people in every locale and every epoch. They have always wondered whether the hints of transcendence in everyday experience may be pointers provided by God about death's higher purpose. The intuition keeps popping up that death, frightful though it be and whatever its origins, may be God's means of embracing us. So we might ask what clues God may have planted in our nature and our history to point to this divine invitation to find God in death.

Fortunately we do not have to look beyond what is already very familiar to us. I am speaking of how God speaks in our history and how God speaks to our hearts.

The words God uses to speak in our history are not nouns and verbs. They are people—the self-transcending and faith-filled people who have gone before us, as well as those whom we honor in our midst today: Abraham and Sarah, Isaac and Rebecca, Jacob and Leah. Isaiah, Jeremiah, Ezekiel; Ruth and Esther. Confucius, Chuang Tzu, Lao Tzu, Buddha, Jesus. Augustine, Thomas Aquinas, Martin Luther. Mahatma Gandhi, Mother Teresa, Dag Hammarskjold . . . If these persons are God's "words," then their communities are God's "sentences," and, strung out along the line of time, their interweaving in history are God's "story." Where authors tried to write that story, we have scriptures that we hold sacred. Yet whether written or merely spoken, the story tells us that death is not the end and that God and death are intimately related.

Besides individuals and their histories, everything in the universe is a type of "word" from God. Often the world around us provides metaphors—the meat and potatoes of preachers seeking to console and encourage: God is like a king or a lover, a master or a servant. God is like the wind, blowing where it will, or a lamp in a nitch to light our way. Metaphors are also the fare of theologians seeking to understand what faith holds true: God is like a shamrock, with each leaf a "person." Or God "utters" the Son the way the mind expresses an appreciation, and God "welcomes" that Son the way the heart welcomes what it appreciates.

But beyond metaphors, the created universe is a word of God in yet a more profound sense. The very incompleteness of each mortal thing reveals God to the inquiring heart by a kind of *pointing*. Wherever we have unanswered questions, we can still affirm that the particular and concrete meaning of this situation at this time will find its fulfillment in God. Not merely in the sense that God creates everything and so carries the big plan in a divine mind, but more in the sense that God *by nature* expresses the divine self, the divine essence, so that each thing reveals the spit and image of God. God is a lover, not a toymaker. God is not creating plays for divine entertainment. No, to those who believe that it is God's essence to love, it seems unavoidable to regard creation as God's irrevocable gift of self, so that the facets of meaning that we glimpse in creation around us are reflections of meaning in the essence of God.

It is practically impossible to contemplate this without imagining that we experience the passing of time after we die. As we saw, there are dangers in this image and, in any case, we have no evidence whatsoever that time continues for us through death. On the other hand, it would be foolish not to contemplate it at all. So, without making any claim about a life that follows this one in time, we need to think of "before/after" and "then/now" not along a timeline but merely with regard to the transformation of our lives that death brings.

Where people of faith spend their lives seeing God in all things, after the transformation of death they will see all things in God. They will see it not as a collection of individual things but in the actual complex and palpable manner that everything played in history. To put it starkly, the God we do not know, that mysterious divine beyond our comprehension, has at least given us the data that in the final revelation will make sense. In the meantime, before our final transformation, what we see and touch, the people we care for and struggle with, the stories we tell and the history we make are all data on the Divine.

This is true of all the attractive things we know. Harmonious situations, beautiful people, gorgeous scenes easily point to God the designer and draw us to seek the mystery behind such beauty. But it is also true of the unattractive. Wretched situations, hateful people, and ecological dumps also point to God in the way they automatically raise the question in us about what might be missing here, much as tragic operas do.

While most believers will acknowledge that the meaning of everything will be found in God, fewer expect that the meaning of each particular will be found in God *retaining its particularity*. For example, the difficult time a friend has with her teenage son these days has only provisional meaning. In twenty years they might look back on it with a more benign understanding than they have now. All the more so when they are finally wrapped in God through death. Then they will understand what every annoyance and every hesitant peace offering meant in the context of God's purposes in history. Likewise, in much of what was said above, we looked at individuals in community and in history and concluded that somehow these reveal the true God to us. We acknowledge that in the essence of God we will find what our personalities, communities, and histories really meant in time. It is by believing that the significance of any one thing, any one person or event, will be completed rather than lost in God, that we give our hearts reason to hope.

While I have been brought up a believing Christian, I cannot believe that God abandons everyone else. What Jesus is to me, what Muhammad and the Koran are to the Muslim, what physical nature is to some, and the Cloud of Unknowing is to others—all converge on a single divine reality. They all speak of the one God and of our one, mortal humanity. But they speak to us in circumstances that will never be forgotten but rather woven into one story that makes complete sense. It is in the very particularity of everything on earth that the meaning and presence of God reside, and such self-expression in love will not be taken back.

These "words" of God—the saintly people, the metaphors, the existential pointers of good and bad situations—are not the only kind of word God speaks. There is that other "word" of God in our hearts. None of the "words" external to us would have any meaning without this other, internal "word." Because we find ourselves incessantly curious, naturally wondering, full of more questions than we could ever answer, we cannot help acknowledging that the search for God in death and life is itself an inner word that says "Seek and ye shall find." No matter how confusing life gets, we seek clarity. No matter how steep the climb, we seek a plateau. No matter how firmly we try to secure our egotism with the cement of self-serving rationalizations, conscience peeps through the cracks like stubborn grass seeking light.

This internal word is a kind of love. It is really the only kind of love. Some religions so exalt God that they cut themselves off from any kind of intimate presence of God in human hearts. Others, however, have taken a mighty leap by affirming that the love in our hearts is not merely a gift *from* God; it is the gift *of* God. God *is* the love in our hearts. Certainly, our hearts are full of false loves too, and so we need regular discernment to sift out the true. But even in the most Godhating persons, love stirs; they go to some lengths to suppress that love perhaps, but most of those who live long enough finally give up. They repent of their past and listen more attentively to what Gandhi called the "still, small voice" in the heart. From that moral conversion, there is still an intellectual conversion awaiting them when they consider that the whole world is quite a different place than the one they imagined. The world becomes the place where we can always count on the presence of a divine love, of a love beyond our nature, to make its presence felt in some person, in some community, at some historical point.

In our earlier chapters, we looked at the presence of hope in human hearts as clues to the character of the divine. Hope has turned out to be far more than clues. Hope may be divine love itself as it extrudes into time. Hope is just possibly the spirit of God on the move in history, the engine of its redemption. Hope stands at the transition between human consciousness and divine grace. Our hope in life-through-death cannot point to evidence for its justification; indeed, the evidence of cadavers suggests to some that death may be the end. Rather the justification of hope lies in its transcendent effects. We trust hope because it is so closely connected to the overflowing of love in human hearts. And love occurs everywhere. All great religious traditions point to love as our highest calling and most noble achievement.

It is important to realize that we did not have to be like this. In the all-encompassing design of the universe, of all things physical and spiritual, it so happens that the entities we call "people" simultaneously seek the ultimate direction of things and at times represent the highest achievements of that direction. Just as we experience the inner words of wonder, hope, and love, we become the outer words of incarnate value, walking proof that human success depends on love.

These profound mysteries of God and history, of life and death, beckon us through the outer word in our histories and the inner word in our hearts. These two "words" are God's self-gift to us, drawing us into mystery by these two delicate cords of love.

Death is necessary for both words. Death gives the inner word of wonder its driving character, urging us to make something of ourselves and to appreciate the world's beauties in the span of time allotted us. Without death, if life were endless, wonder would be just wander, desire would be fickle, love would be eternally adolescent. Regarding the outer word, death gives it its historical character, rendering every event unrevisable and permanently significant. Without death, if people were perpetually protean, Moses would be adding commandments, Lincoln would reconsider slavery, and Anne Frank would edit her diary.

The shadow of death cast on every human event—indeed every event in the universe—reveals the silhouette of God. Death is there in God in the same double-word pattern. The inner word that God speaks in our hearts—the movements of curiosity, hope, trust, desire, care, welcome—are the occurrence in time and space of God's getting beyond, God's own self-transcendence, God expanding, God dying to alternatives. And the outer word that God speaks in our history—the prophets, saints, angels, sacred books, lush and awesome nature—are the manifestation in time and space of God's commitment to this and not that, God's being of such a nature and not otherwise, God's eternal death to alternatives and irrevocable, self-sacrificing promise to humanity.

Death is not just God's *idea* of loving us. Death is God's *self* loving us. When, in that time of no whens, we see God, we will see death with all its mystery revealed.

A CLOSING MEDITATION AND PRAYER

"It's really very easy. You mix diced frozen potatoes, butter, sour cream, cream of celery soup, grated cheddar cheese, salt and pepper, and top it with crushed potato chips. Bake it at 350° for an hour—uncovered so the top is nice and crispy."

"And it's practical for a lunch after a funeral. So many relatives and friends show up. And don't worry if you make too much, you can always divvy up the leftovers or eat them yourself. It is important to have a dish you can make quick, because there's so many other things to do when someone dies."

"You certainly don't want to try a quiche, which may not turn out, or guacamole, which not everyone likes."

It is apparent from this typical advice that when death comes it is important to make things reliable. People don't like surprises at funerals. Out-of-town visitors need to know exactly where they're staying and where to go to offer condolences. If any preachers are involved, they had better not say anything too cute or too abstract. We would rather hear something wholly forgettable than something memorably gauche.

Bereavement needs the ordinary and the common. Death has blasted a hole in the middle of our lives and we need to put as much in order as we can. So we surround our grief with familiar food and familiar people. We encircle it with what we know. This is because we fear, we know, that during the weeks to come death will continue ravaging the familiar anyway. "She used to do the shopping." "He was so good at cooking." "I miss his snoring at night." "We have to move; I can't stand this house without her."

And so death reminds us of what it really means to have someone around. We hug our fellow survivors more often, and with more passion. We want the *commonplace* because, as the word suggests, it places us in common with those we care for at the level of our shared mortality. We want the *familiar* because, as that word suggests, we are deeply one family in this life-unto-death.

After a funeral, we marinate the familiar. We spend more time keeping quiet, not thinking about anything, not making plans. A widow sits by her kitchen window, unmoored, drifting, simply letting herself realize that here she is. She didn't have to be. The robins outside and the grapefruit on her plate are strangely wonderful in the way they seem to be what they are without the complications of a mind seduced by mystery.

Are humans the only things in the universe that grieve? What a tremendous weight of spirit must we be carrying if matters of the spirit weigh so heavily on our hearts! What unexplored powers forcibly turn our faces toward mystery! And yet these profound spiritual depths in us have a hankering for a potato casserole!

Kind God, look at us: We are surrounded with the familiar! When we come before you in your beatific welcome, when we have submitted finally to the total demands of death, will you really take us as we are? Will you really accept the plain truth that we prefer our hair done a certain way, that we revel in dancing, that we always dig for our favorite knife in the kitchen drawer?

If so, then we hereby notify you in advance what we expect. We want the painful bereavements we have suffered to be healed, of course. But there's more—something without which we will not feel totally at peace. We want to cling to everything we have ever relished—popcorn, peanut butter, English muffins, the old couch in the basement where we used to read, the wave-worn brick we brought back from the shores of Lake Ontario, the kitchen table that saw so many tears, of both hurt and humor. Remember this, kind God, when you see us grievers dig into our potato casseroles with their crispy potato-chip toppings.

THAT DAY

Let me close with a symbolic representation that can barely approximate the reality.

On that day, everything meaningful will be at hand. The entire human community stretching across the globe and down the aeons will have gathered. Each of us will sit at table with everyone to whom we were ever linked. For myself, I expect to see Jesus at the head. For those who have not known the Jesus of history, God's timeless word will be clearly spoken and clearly heard—Krishna to some, Isis and

Osiris to others; Moses, Elijah and all the prophets to some; the spirit of the Koran to others.

As we celebrate, I expect to notice that Jesus still bears nail scars on his hands and feet. There's a scar on his ribs. But they are beautiful scars. Each one radiant. The crucified Christ and the compassionate Christ remain eternally the same reality.

And then we see, in delightful clarity, dazzling scars on everyone—every cut incurred, every death undergone, every act of killing ill-conceived inspirations, every event in which we died to enrich our brothers and sisters.

We will see Muslims and Hindus, Buddhists and Shintoists, Taoists and believers of every known stripe, all recognizing in each other a common wonder, all recognizing in God's word and spirit the object and source of their best desires.

We will see Matty Ventresca, with his adoptive parents Brian and Gina and his sister Kim, as well as with his natural parents, whose wounds will explain why they had to give him up. Matty will cradle a snake in his arms—Innocence in triumph over our Original Tempter. His heart is lopsided, his lungs and kidneys scarified, but he shines like the morning sun he loves.

Our wounds are our glory, and our only glory.

Looking around, we see the spirit of God in everyone, quivering like fire, revealing them to be an everlasting part of God's historical word. That word, that Christ, is incomplete without us, for, in the words of Gerard Manley Hopkins,

> Christ plays in ten thousand places,
> Lovely in limbs, and lovely in eyes
> Not his to the Father through the features
> Of our faces.

We see God face to face, not God as someone other than the Spirit or the Word, but God whose radiance is the Word, whose welcome is the Spirit.

The family is proud and happy.

All is well.

We ourselves see that all manner of thing is well.

Sources

Here are the sources of the chief materials used in the text:

PROLOG

In 1992, my wife, Dorothy, and I were vacationing in California and happened to notice a charming little church north of San Francisco near Bolinas. We stopped to walk around and came upon a cemetery behind the church and the wonderful grave marker depicted on the cover. I took a picture of it and, later, made a sketch, which I stored with other drawings and forgot about it.

Then, in late winter of 1994, prompted by the death of my friend Leo, then the sudden death of Dorothy's aunt, and then by a request from my friend, Mary Jo, for a reflective book on death, I started writing down a few thoughts. The few grew to many. When I realized that others might benefit from these reflective pieces, I decided to make a book of it.

It seemed appropriate to try to reach the Ventresca family to let them know my intentions. So, owing to the marvel of modern communications and databases, I was talking to Matty's mother, Gina, on my second phone call. She told me Matty's story and later sent me many materials and photographs. Among them was the story and letter written by Brian, Matty's father. I am writing this a day after visiting the Ventrescas in California. Something drew me back. Or *someone*.

PREFACE

For a summary view of how various religions understand death, see Kenneth Kramer, *The Sacred Art of Dying: How World Religions Understand Death* (New York: Paulist, 1988).

1. The Myths About Death

The quote beginning, "Rage, rage . . ." comes from Dylan Thomas' "Do Not Go Gentle Into That Good Night." See *The Poems of Dylan Thomas* (New York: New Directions, 1971) pp. 207-208.

For Karl Rahner's views on death, see "On Christian Dying," *Theological Investigations 7* (New York: Herder & Herder, 1971) 285-293; esp. 287. Similar observations can be found in "Theological Considerations Concerning the Moment of Death," *Theological Investigations 11* (Baltimore: Helican Press, 1961) 320.

For Peter's first recorded homily, see Acts 2:14-36.

2. Our Many Voices

See Elizabeth Kubler-Ross, *On Death and Dying* (New York: Macmillan, 1969); Ernest Becker, *The Denial of Death* (New York: The Free Press, 1973).

The quote, "all shall be well . . . ," from Dame Julian of Norwich, can be found in *The Revelation of Divine Love: In 16 Showings Made to Dame Julian of Norwich* (Ligouri, MO.: Triumph Books, 1977), p. 109 (Chapter 32). The message, however, is found throughout her writings.

Material on Mesopotamian thought is taken from *Gilgamesh, A Verse Narrative*, by Herbert Mason. Boston: Houghton Mifflin, 1971.

Material on Loatse is from *The Wisdom of Laotse* tr., Lin Yutang (New York: The Modern Library, 1948), Book 5, "The Conduct of Life," section 50.4-50.5.

Material on Job is from *The Jerusalem Bible* (Garden City N: Doubleday, 1966), 10:1-7;18-22; 14:12-22;19:23-29.

Material from Chandogya Upanishad is taken from *The Upanishads*, tr. Juan Mascaro (Baltimore: Penguin, 1965), sections 3.18.1 and 8.1.

Material from the Gita is taken from *The Bhagavad Gita*, tr. Eliot Deutsch. New York: Holt Rinehart and Winston, 1968. See parts XVIII, VII and VIII, in that order. Gender exclusive language has been changed.

The story of the Buddha is recounted by the Buddhist teacher Nagarjuna. Cited by Clive Erricker in his *Buddhism* (Chicago: NTC Publishers Group, 1995) with reference to *Buddhist Studies Review*, Vol. 4, no. 2 1987, p. 106.

Material on Buddhist monks is from *Path of Purification* by Bhadantacarya Buddhaghosa. (Kandy, Sri Lanka: Buddhist Publication Society, Inc., 1979) Book 8, "Description of Concentration" para. 41 and "The Eight Ways" para. 15.

The text from the *Acts of the Apostles* is the author's translation from the Greek, with assistance from Dennis Hamm, S.J.

Material on Islamic thought is the author's translation, relying on *The Holy Qur'an. With English Translation & Commentary*. Vol. 5 (Translator Abdullah Yushf Ali) (Lahore, Pakistan: Sh. Muhammad Ashraf Publishers, 1934) (England: Tilford, Surray: Islam International Publications Ltd., 1988), Chapter 50, 4-12, 16-23.

3. The Image of God in Death

Bernard Lonergan discusses the priority of the world order to each individual within it in "The Natural Desire to See God," *Collection* (New York: Herder & Herder, 1976) p. 88.

"My power is at its best in weakness." See 2 Cor 12:9.

"I will give you your life as a prize of war." See RSV, Jeremiah 45:5.

I credit Bernard Lonergan for explaining the concrete nature of the good and for demonstrating that conscience is the ultimate human source for laws. It clarified many questions I had about my own experience. A concise account of his views can be found in his *Method in Theology* (Herder & Herder, 1972), chapter 2 (pp. 27-55) A more descriptive account can be found in his *Topics in Education*, Vol. 10 of Collected Works of Bernard Lonergan (University of Toronto Press, 1993) pp. 26-33.

In a number of writings, I have described Ignatius' theology of history in more depth. See "Extremism in Ignatius of Loyola," *Review for Religious* 45/3 (May-June, 1986) pp. 345-355; *Spiritual Exercises for Today* (HarperSanFrancisco, 1991) pp. 59-67; *Spiritual Mentoring* (HarperSanFrancisco, 1991) pp. 60-83; "The Cultural Milieus of the Spiritual Exercises" in J. Dister, ed., *A New Introduction to the Spiritual Exercises of St. Ignatius* (Michael Glazier, 1993) pp. 11-24.

The quote from Aquinas is from his *Scriptum super libros Sententiarum IV*, 38.2.4 q.a. 3. See also *IV*, 27.1.2 q.a. 4 ad 3; *IV*, 27.3.3. Chapter 18.

For Lonergan's explanation of the two kinds of awareness, see *Method in Theology* (New York: Herder & Herder, 1972) pp. 7-8 and the leads in its index under "presence." See also "Religious Experience" in *A Third Collection* (New York: Paulist, 1985) pp. 116-117.

Thomas Aquinas often relies on Aristotle's distinction between *what* and *whether*. See Aquinas' *In Aristotelis libros Posteriorum analyticorum*, 2, lect. 1. See also, Bernard Lonergan's *Topics in Education*, Vol. 10 of *The Collected Works of Bernard Lonergan* (Toronto: University of Toronto Press, 1993), p. 53.

4. The Law of Care

For a scientific view of the evolution of spirit within the heart of the evolution of matter, see *The Universe Story: From the Primordial Flaring Forth to the Ecozoic Era*, by Brian Swimme and Thomas Berry (San Francisco: HarperSanFrancisco, 1992).

For more on Hegel's philosophy of history (and other major thinkers) see Karl Löwith, *Meaning in History* (Chicago: University of Chicago Press, 1949).

For the idea of a "second naiveté," see Paul Ricoeur, *Interpretation Theory* (Fort Worth, Texas: Texas Christian University Press, 1976), p. 44; and *Symbolism of Evil* (Boston: Beacon Press, 1967), pp. 350-357.

"Though our outer person is falling into decay, the inner person is renewed day by day. For the present light afflictions, which are soon over, train us for the carrying of a weight of eternal glory that is out of all proportion to them" (2 Cor 4:16-17).

"You have in you one who is greater than anyone in the world." See *The Jerusalem Bible*, 1 Jn 4:4.

5. Voices of Redemption

We might note that most other major religions besides Islam, Judaism, and Christianity underscore how death is indifferent to social status. Hinduism depicts Krishna as guiding Arjuna, a soldier, whom he instructs in the ways of self-forgetfulness. In Buddhism, Siddhartha was born a prince but through progressive enlightenments, came to feel a total compassion toward all creatures. Confucius taught that disciplined and virtuous behavior are the only aspects of life that any person need attend to, ignoring fame and speculation about the afterlife altogether.

6. Walking in the Shadow of Death

For references to Leviathan in the Hebrew Bible, see Job 41:1; Ps 74:14; 104:26; Isa 27:1.

See *Spiritual Exercises of St. Ignatius*, particularly the rules for understanding spirits (inspirations) and the rules for scruples. For the source of Ignatius' "Two Standards" vision of history, see "De duobus Dominus at duabus civitatibus et diversis aliis rebus" by Werner, Abbot of St. Blase of the Black Forest (d. 1126) in *Los Origenes de los Ejercicios Espiritualis de S. Ignacio de Loyola*, ed. P. Arturo Codina (Barcelona: Biblioteca Balmes, 1926) 287-89.

For an updated version of rules for understanding inspirations, see my "Dynamics of Spirit" and "Dynamics of Story" in *Spiritual Exercises for Today* (San Francisco: HarperSanFrancisco, 1991), pp. 161-175.

See James 4:1 for his view on how disputes between people arise from disputes within them.

"The Lord is very near. There is no need to worry." See Philippians 4:5. The quotation from the *Bhagavad Gita* can be found in chapter 18, paragraphs 64-66.

Regarding material on how more people choose the manner of their death: "Of the 2.2 million annual deaths in the United States, 80 percent occur in health care facilities; in roughly 1.5 million of these cases, death is preceded by some explicit decision about stopping or not starting medical treatment. Thus, death in America is not only medically managed, but its timing is also increasingly subject to deliberate choice." From Leon R. Kass, "Is There a Right to Die?" *Hastings Center Report* 23/1 (Jan/Feb 93) 34.

"Dementia is estimated to affect from 7 to 20 percent of persons between the ages of seventy-five and eighty-four, and 25 to 47 percent of persons above that age." Cited by Rebecca Dresser and Peter J. Whitehouse in "The Incompetent Patient on the Slippery Slope," *Hastings Center Report* 24/4 (Jul/Aug 94) 7. These statistics, bolstered by people's personal experience of aging parents, have led many people to believe that dementia is "natural" for older people and, therefore, to a neglect of the their otherwise preventable problems. Dementia is a disease that is curable in many cases; it is also predictable for most people through simple tests. The point is that too many doctors and patients are not alarmed enough to take steps to prevent or forestall its onset.

Many moralists have traditionally found justification that extraordinary means do not have to be taken to preserve a life. While the majority of medical ethicists today agree, there is confusion about what is meant by "extraordinary means," particularly when technologies once considered rare and expensive are now commonplace and cheap. The meaning of the original doctrine was identical to the long-accepted principle of proportionality, namely, that the benefits of any medical intervention should outweigh the drawbacks. The term "extraordinary means" is not a principle to be used to justify a decision; it is merely a way of expressing that decision. The justification lies in balancing drawbacks and benefits. A hospital ethicist, therefore, cannot object to withholding ordinary nutrition and hydration by saying these means are not "extraordinary." The question is whether the benefits of withholding (usually a shortening of a painful and/or vegetative life) outweigh the drawbacks (death). See James J. McCartney, "The

Development of the Doctrine of Ordinary and Extraordinary Means of Preserving Life in Catholic Moral Theology Before the Karen Quinlan Case," *Linacre Quarterly*, August 1980, 215-224; cited by Thomas Garrett et al., *Health Care Ethics* (Englewood, New Jersey: Prentice Hall, 1989), pp. 58-59. See also, Richard McCormick, S.J., "Some Early Reactions to *Veritas Splendor*" *Theological Studies* (55) 1994, 504.

7. Meeting Death with Faith

The poem is from *Poems and Prose of Gerard Manley Hopkins* (Baltimore: Penguin Books, 1953), p. 57. It is untitled, but begins, "As kingfishers catch fire . . ."; I have replaced an archaism for readability.

Index

Afterlife, 7, 13ff, 32, 48, 50, 63, 81, 116, 164
Allah, 119
Aquinas, Thomas, 74, 173
Aristotle, 79, 173
Arjuna, 38f, 144
Assurance, 156
Atman, 9, 36
Augustine, 87, 136

Baptism, 133f
Brahman, 35ff
Buddha, Buddhism, 40ff, 135
Burke, William, 132

Care, Law of, 85ff
Catholic, ix, 73, 76
Certitude, 127, 129, 156, 163
Chuang-Tzu, 29ff
Cloud of Unknowing, 165
Colossians, 135
Community, 64, 72, 83, 90ff, 97, 100, 117, 148
Comte, August, 65
Confucius, vii, 13, 29
Conscience, 74f, 80, 117, 154ff, 165

Consciousness, 91
Contemplation, 62, 107ff, 162
Conviction, 156
Creationist, 58f
Creativity, 124

David, 45, 47
D-Day, 145
Dementia, 150
Discern, 136f, 145
Dilthey, Wilhelm, viii

Egyptian, vii
Emerson, Ralph Waldo, 72
Endiku, 26ff
Entropy, 56, 88
Ethics, 126, 151, 155
Evolutionist, 58f

Faith, viii, ix, 21f, 34, 46f, 54, 77, 82f, 105, 120, 134, 143f, 157, 163ff
Forgiveness, 37, 80ff, 105, 124, 159
Frailty, 68f, 83
Freedom, 10f, 144

Gandhi, 163, 165
Gilgamesh, vii, 13, 26ff, 104
Gita, Bhagavad, vii, 9, 37ff, 144
Greek, vii, 13

Hammarskjöld, Dag, 163
Heaven, 15, 25, 79f
Hebrew, vii, 13, 98, 155
Hegel, Georg Wilhelm Friedrich, viii, 31, 89, 174
Hell, 79, 97
Hindu, vii, 9, 35ff, 135
Historiography, 146
History, 60, 66, 72, 77, 89, 92, 103ff, 129, 148, 155, 158
Hope, 57, 62, 82, 97, 165f
Hopkins, Gerard Manley, 169, 176

Identity, 141f
Ignatius Loyola, 94, 99, 137f, 173f
Immortality, 8, 11ff, 63f, 100f, 114
Inspiration, 47, 83, 132ff, 159
Islamic, 48, 98

Jesus, 19, 45ff, 120, 128, 144, 155, 163
Jewish, 147
Job, 31ff
Judeo-Christian, 85
Julian of Norwich, 26, 172

Koran, vii, 47ff, 100, 135, 165, 169
Krishna, 9, 144, 168

Laotse, 29f, 135
Life support (artificial), 149
Lonergan, Bernard, 173
Love, 83, 101, 110ff, 157, 165

Luke, 45ff
Luther, Martin, 99

Macmurray, John, 132
Marx, Karl, 65
Mary, 73
Mesopotamian, vii, 13
Metaphor, 79, 83, 164
Moral, 32, 97, 117. 125ff, 133
Mortal (death), 116
Muhammad, 52, 119
Muslim, vii, 47ff, 119, 165, 169
Mystery, 61f, 83, 107, 123, 166f

New Testament, vii, 20, 135
Niehuhr, Reinhold, 97

Originalist, 64ff

Paul, 15, 32, 68
Physical (death), 117
Plato, vii
Prayer, 99
Present, 91f
Progressivist, 64ff
Proposition, 18, 24, 31, 39, 83, 106
Protestant, 74, 127
Providence, 53, 77
Purgatory, 37, 78ff

Quinlan, Karen Ann, 125

Rahner, Karl, 9, 172
Redeems, 93, 113ff, 123ff
Redemption, 93, 107, 113ff, 123
Regret, 40
Reincarnation, 35

Resurrection, 19f, 45ff, 123
Ricoeur, Paul, 16, 174

Sartre, Jean-Paul, 72, 97
Science, ix, 53, 56, 58ff, 83, 85, 88, 108, 146, 174
Sheol, 32f, 46
Simpson, O. J., 118ff
Sinatra, Frank, 139
Socrates, vii, 14
Sufi, 119

Taoism, 135
Teresa of Avila, 99
Thatcher, Margaret, 72
Thomas, Dylan, 172

Toynbee, viii
Tradition, 47, 72, 154, 155
Transforming (death), 117
Trinity, 100f

Upanishads, vii, 9, 35ff

Valkali, 39ff
Vatican, 76
Ventresca, Matty, 1ff, 7f, 22, 26, 43, 49f, 50, 55f, 66, 70, 86, 103, 114, 169

Word, 127ff, 163, 165f

Books of Interest in the Death, Value and Meaning Series

Series Editor: John D. Morgan

The Magical Thoughts of Grieving Children: Treating Children with Complicated Mourning and Advice for Parents
By James A. Fogarty, Ed.D.

Death Without Notice
By Sandra Helene Straub

Meeting the Needs of Our Clients Creatively: The Impact of Art and Culture on Caregiving
Editor: John D. Morgan

Grief and the Healing Arts: Creativity as Therapy
Editor: Sandra L. Bertman

When a Child Has Been Murdered: Ways You Can Help the Grieving Parents
By Bonnie Hunt Conrad

The Death of an Adult Child: A Book for and About Bereaved Parents
By Jeanne Webster Blank

When Dreams Don't Work: Professional Caregivers and Burnout
By Ronna Jevne and Donna Reilly Williams

Heavenly Hurts: Surviving AIDS Related Deaths and Losses
By Sandra Jacoby Klein

All Kinds of Love: Experiencing Hospice
By Carolyn Jaffe and Carol H. Ehrlich

Readings in Thanatology
Editor: John D. Morgan

Mending the Torn Fabric: For Those Who Grieve and Those Who Want to Help Them
By Sarah Brabant

Widower: When Men Are Left Alone
By Scott Campbell and Phyllis R. Silverman

Awareness of Mortality
Editor: Jeffrey Kauffman

Ethical Issues in the Care of the
Dying and Bereaved Aged
Editor: John D. Morgan

Fading Away: The Experience of Transition in Families with
Terminal Illness
*Editors: Betty Davies, Joanne Chekryn Reimer,
Pamela Brown and Nola Martens*

Last Rites: The Work of the Modern Funeral Director
By: Glennys Howarth

Perspectives on College Student Suicide
By Ralph L. V. Rickgarn

What Will We Do?
Preparing a School Community to Cope with Crises
Editor: Robert G. Stevenson

Personal Care in an Impersonal World:
A Multidimensional Look at Bereavement
Editor: John D. Morgan

Death and Spirituality
Editor: Kenneth J. Doka with John D. Morgan

Spiritual, Ethical and Pastoral Aspects
of Death and Bereavement
Editors: Gerry R. Cox and Ronald J. Fundis

Greeting the Angels:
An Imaginal View of the Mourning Process
By Greg Mogenson

Beyond the Innocence of Childhood – 3 Volume Set
Editors: David W. Adams and Eleanor J. Deveau

Volume 1
Factors Influencing Children and Adolescents'
Perceptions and Attitudes Toward Death

Volume 2
Helping Children and Adolescents
Cope with Life-Threatening Illness and Dying

Volume 3
Helping Children and Adolescents Cope with
Death and Bereavement